MASTERING MEMORY

MASTERING MEMORY

75 MEMORY HACKS
FOR SUCCESS IN SCHOOL, WORK & LIFE

BRAD ZUPP, MEMORY COACH & RECORD-SETTING MEMORY ATHLETE

ALTHEA
PRESS

Interior Designer: Carol Angstadt
Cover Designer: Michael Patti
Art Producer: Sara Feinstein
Editor: Melissa Valentine
Production Editor: Ashley Polikoff
Illustrations © istockphoto

ISBN: Print 978-1-64152-286-1 | eBook 978-1- 64152-287-8

Contents

PART 1: Life

PART 2: School and Personal Growth

PART 3: Work

FOCUS

CREATE

TRY

QUESTION

DETECT

PLAY

CONNECT

NUMBER

IMAGE

REVIEW

Introduction

DO YOU OFTEN find yourself walking into rooms and forgetting why you're there? Do you misplace your phone, glasses, or other important items? Do you forget what your friends and family tell you? Do you have difficulty remembering facts and figures? If so, you aren't alone; I can relate. I have never had an exceptional memory; I have always had trouble remembering names and numbers. As I got older, my ability to remember things has gotten worse—until one day I had enough. "Can an ordinary guy actually improve his memory?" I wondered. I decided to find out.

I researched, read, and experimented with everything from meditation and exercise to taking vitamins and getting more sleep. Some strategies worked; others didn't. But overall the result was that my memory improved! Surprisingly, learning memory strategies was fun. It wasn't like the drudgery of schoolwork and rote memorization that I'd expected. I found tools and techniques that were not only easy but enjoyable to use.

Being able to remember more information was so enjoyable that I started to dabble in memory competitions. Yes, there are people in the world who have made memorizing a competitive sport—and I became one of them! As in any sport or endeavor, the more I practiced, the better I got. Eventually I was competing at the international level.

At one event I broke the record for the United States that year. The following year, I broke my own record. I could perfectly recall a list of numbers spoken at the rate of one per second for over two minutes. I could also memorize the order of a deck of shuffled playing cards in less than 60 seconds, the order of 1,200 binary digits in 30 minutes, 11.5 decks of playing cards in an hour, 117 names and faces in 15 minutes, and more. Of course, my day-to-day memory improved as well. I remembered more of what my wife said, I did better at work, and I could even remember the names of people I met. My memory was better and my life was, too.

What I found more interesting than my success at these competitions was that almost everyone else I met at these events had a similar story to mine: They were concerned about their poor memories, decided to improve their minds, and . . . it worked! They were able to train themselves to remember more.

As a memory athlete and coach for thousands of students, from as young as grade three to adults and senior citizens, I've proven again and again that these techniques work. If you follow the simple steps in this book your memory will improve, too. Each part of this book—Life, School and Personal Growth, and Work—has 25 practical memory hacks. I encourage you to read the book straight through to get the most out of it, because foundational techniques are included with many of the hacks. However, if you have a pressing need, feel free to go directly to that solution.

The techniques are different from the type of rote memorization many of us have used in the past. They may even seem weird, time consuming, or unbelievable. It's common to find a technique strange until you try it. So don't just read this book. Pick a technique and put all your effort into practicing the hack—you might be surprised at how well it works for you! You *can* have a good memory. Using these techniques will help you work *with* your mind instead of *against* it. You can do this! Your memory will improve . . . and so will your life.

PART

1

Life

These first 25 memory hacks lay the foundation for more complex methods and techniques to come. The techniques in this section are incredibly powerful and will help with many common situations where we struggle to remember. To begin with, as you read through this part, choose one or two hacks that interest you and put them into practice.

[1] The Three Essential Memory Steps

MOST PEOPLE THINK that remembering happens during a moment in time: We hear something and then we either remember it or we forget it. But memory is more complicated than that. Remembering anything requires these three essential steps (FAR):

1 **F**ocus on the information.

2 **A**rrange the material in your mind.

3 **R**etrieve it when you need it.

To go FAR with your efforts to improve your memory, you need to follow through on all three of these steps. If you skip one, you won't be able to recall what you want to when you need to. The starting place for improving your memory is to identify which of these steps may be tripping you up. Once you have identified your problem area, you will know where you need to concentrate your effort as you work through this book.

THE TECHNIQUE : Identify Problem Areas

For this hack, you'll need to spend a few minutes considering your memory. Grab a pen and paper. You don't need a fancy journal—the back of an envelope or a piece of scrap paper is fine. When you analyze your recent memory problems in writing, you can pinpoint which of the steps is your biggest concern. In my experience, many memory issues are the result of skipping step 1, not focusing on the information. We often do so many things at once that our attention is scattered and our natural memory can't function properly. That's not always the case, though, so let's look at your situation.

HOW TO DO IT

Take a moment to think about a recent memory issue. What did you forget? On your scrap paper, jot down a word or two that summarizes the event or problem. For example, "Forgot anniversary," "Blanked out on big test," or "Forgot deadline at work."

Now, think about the time surrounding the memory issue. What led up to it, what happened when you tried to recall the information, and what happened after? Answer the following questions:

1   Did you not focus closely enough for the information to settle into your mind when you heard, read, or saw the information? In other words, did you fail to pay attention?

2   Did the information settle into your mind but then got jumbled along with other information you had stored?

3   Did you have the information stored in your mind, but when it came time to recall it you "blanked out"?

Beneath the word(s) that summarize the event, jot down which of the three steps tripped you up: 1) Focusing on the information; 2) Arranging the material in the mind; or 3) Retrieving it when you need it. Now, repeat this activity for at least two more times when you had memory problems. Then add the possible reasons for each. Here's an example:

> *Forgot anniversary (step 2)—Knew date but didn't have it on my mind because I was thinking about other things.*
>
> *Blanked out on big test (step 3)—Knew information but forgot the material under pressure.*
>
> *Forgot deadline at work (step 1)—Didn't remember that boss changed deadline.*

In this example there are three areas to work on. Your list may reveal that you need to work on all three areas, too. Maybe there's a pattern of having information go "in one ear and out the other" (step 1), having so much going on in your mind that you have trouble remembering (step 2), or finding that you are stressed and unable to access information at the moment you need it (step 3). Whatever the case may be for you, knowing which area(s) need your attention will help you as you begin your memory improvement journey!

[2] A Better Memory Every Morning

WE HAVE SO many things to remember each day, including the names of people we meet, upcoming deadlines, daily tasks, conversations with the people in our lives, and much more. It can seem overwhelming, especially if we already struggle to remember well. Waking up each morning may even bring a sense of dread: "How will I embarrass myself today with my bad memory?" Instead of living in fear or concern, you can immediately improve your memory and see growth every day. You just need to make a few small changes in your habits and attitudes to begin growing your memory abilities.

THE TECHNIQUE : Take Care of Your Body and Mind

You may be sabotaging your memory without knowing it. A few simple life changes will make all the difference. Taking care of your body and mind yields huge memory results with minimal effort. We often get so busy or stressed out that we stop doing what we know is good for us. Taking care of your body and mind will give your natural memory what it needs to work for you again. While this may seem easier said than done, read these suggestions with an eye toward what you could do to make positive changes in your life.

HOW TO DO IT

Review the following list of five factors that help support a healthy mind and memory. Choose one or two new habits to incorporate into your routine. Then get to it by taking a few small steps today and tomorrow to start a healthy habit. You're worth it, and your memory will thank you.

1   **GET MORE SLEEP.** Our minds know how to save information and recall it later. We naturally do it all the time. When we get less sleep than we need, however, our minds struggle. Prioritize getting to sleep earlier and sleeping better. Limit screen time, stress, and mental activity before bedtime. This is the number one way many people improve their ability to remember.

2   **DRINK PLENTY OF WATER.** Being dehydrated can impair memory. How much water is right for you? Consult your physician, but a general guideline is six to eight glasses a day.

3   **GET AND STAY PHYSICALLY ACTIVE.** Mental fitness benefits greatly from physical fitness. There is a direct correlation between cardiovascular exercise and a good memory. Consult your physician first, and then walk or do other forms of exercise that are appropriate for your age and physical abilities.

4   **EAT WELL.** We know that we need to eat well for our physical health. Our brain health also relies on getting enough omega-3 fatty acids (try walnuts, salmon, or chia seeds) and antioxidant-rich foods like spinach, almonds, sunflower seeds, blueberries, kale, pecans, strawberries, oranges, and beans. Surely there are a few items here that you enjoy, right? Consult a physician for help choosing the foods that are best for your personal health.

Keep in mind that you may not have to create all new menus. What meals do you eat regularly that you could easily add one of these foods to? I like to add a sprinkle of chia seeds to my oatmeal or into a glass or water. Could you sneak some chopped kale or spinach into your lasagna without noticing?

5   **REDUCE YOUR STRESS LEVEL.** Stress is one of the biggest enemies of memory. Do your mind a favor: Figure out healthy ways to reduce stress, then practice them on a daily basis. Schedule them into your calendar. Some that work for me and my coaching clients include a bath before bed; a slow, relaxing walk before breakfast or after dinner; or a nightly call with a friend who will listen and support you while you do the same for them. (Listening to another's trials and tribulations often makes our problems seem more manageable.)

[3] Remember Where You Left Important Everyday Items

ARE YOU FRUSTRATED by constantly losing your glasses, keys, purse, wallet, phone, or other small items? Do you wander the house looking for things, cursing your bad memory? This is one of the biggest complaints I hear from people both young and old. Many can remember important things like names but constantly lose their glasses. Students can be diligent in doing homework but then don't turn it in because they forget where they put it. If you find yourself misplacing items, this technique is for you.

THE TECHNIQUE : Use Your Imagination

Though we may say, "I forgot where I put my glasses," that statement isn't accurate. The problem isn't that we forgot—it's that we weren't paying attention when we put them down! We put our keys on the counter on the way to wash our hands and then can't find our keys later. We run inside the house to grab something and put our sunglasses on the table by the door. Once we have retrieved what we needed and are back in the car, ready to drive away, we can't find our sunglasses.

If you put items down absentmindedly, how can you bring your focus to the situation? How can you possibly make such inconsequential moments have meaning? With this technique, you'll use your imagination to focus on where you put things so you'll never lose them again.

HOW TO DO IT

1   Think of an object that you lose frequently. Maybe it's your keys, wallet, purse, or phone. Is it only this item, or are there others? Think of the last few times you've "forgotten" and narrow it down to one or two that you frequently misplace. Bring to mind where that item belongs. That's its safe place.

2   Now, for each item, imagine that it has a destructive quality when it's not in its safe place. For example, I think of my keys as so hot that they are glowing red. Whenever I set

them down, I think, "What will happen if I leave them there too long? The table might catch on fire!"

3   Spend 30 seconds trying different visualizations. Imagine your item as hot, cold, wet, painted, or covered in something. For instance, you could picture your item as frozen or wet, leaving behind a puddle or stain. If you prefer color in your imagination, try visualizing the item as green with radioactivity or yellow from being freshly dipped in paint. Is food easier to picture? Think of your phone as having ketchup smeared all over it.

4   Take your item somewhere nearby where it doesn't belong and set it down. Immediately think of how that surface could be damaged. Be creative and exaggerate. Think of an outlandish scenario involving your dangerous item and what it is resting on. Move the item to another surface and repeat the process.

5   Experiment for the rest of today when you put the item down. See how vivid you can make your images. Take a quarter of a second to think, "Oh no, that surface is going to be ruined!" Consider briefly how it would look after being burned, scarred, melted, or splattered.

As silly as this technique sounds, you'll be amazed at the results when you try it. The mind thinks in pictures. You're helping it pay attention in a way it will find amusing, and you'll remember where your items are much better from now on. Make this a game you play every time you handle those (formerly) frequently misplaced items.

TIP | IMPROVE YOUR FOCUS

To immediately start remembering better, stop multitasking! Listen, read, or look with intention at the one thing in front of you to stay in the moment. Give your attention to only one task or person at a time.

[4] Remember If You Unplugged, Turned Off, Closed, and Locked

A JOURNEY OF a thousand miles begins with . . . turning around to make sure you locked the front door. I used to worry that I had left the iron, stove, or oven on, or the doors unlocked. I often doubted myself several minutes after closing the door or turning off the stove, just when it's most inconvenient to double-check. "Did I do actually do it?" I wondered. Using this technique, you'll not only remember to unplug, turn off, lock, or close, you'll remember that you did it, too.

THE TECHNIQUE : Make the Mundane Memorable

This technique helps you remember events that happen frequently enough to be unmemorable but should be remembered. You need to connect your experience of doing the event with something that makes the mundane memorable: singing. You're not a good singer, you say? Even better! An off-key jingle is more memorable than a well-sung song. But if you're around others or feel uncomfortable singing, other noises work just as well.

HOW TO DO IT

1   Pick your biggest concern. Iron? Locked door? Stove? Whether it's hitting the down button on the garage remote, unplugging the iron, or something else, decide that you want to remember doing this task.

2   Make up a song or sound to go along with the action you want to remember doing, and add an identifier such as the day or the weather. Here are a couple of suggestions:

- I sing, "The iron is unplugged on Monday!" in a dramatic, operatic voice as I unplug the iron. Closing the garage door with the remote is similar: "It's a rainy morning, and I've closed the garage!" Using a variety of notes from high to low or low to high is excellent, as is a big crescendo. Make your song lyric in your favorite style: rap, country, pop, or opera. A terrible rendition is fine and even more memorable than a beautifully sung one, so belt it out!

- If songwriting isn't your thing, you can use a noise instead. For instance, to remember that I locked the front door, as I leave, I often jiggle the door knob and think, "Three jiggles Monday morning," counting them as I think it. A hand clap, finger snap, or foot stomp is also effective.

It's important to add an identifier. Without one, I might remember that I sang my little tune but psych myself out thinking, "Wait, maybe I sang that the oven was off yesterday!" and I'd have to go recheck it. When you combine your song/sound with an identifier and then later question yourself, you can quickly recall the song or sound and circumstances, and you'll remember with ease. Your peace of mind will increase, and you'll stop wasting time double-checking yourself.

[5] Remember Names

THERE YOU ARE at a social function or work event. You've just met a person whose name you'd like to remember. Suddenly, though it's only been a second, their name is already gone from your mind. You feel frustrated and embarrassed. Remembering names is an important skill to have. Unfortunately, many people find it a hard skill to master. With this powerful yet simple technique you can easily remember names. From now on, whenever you meet someone and hear their name, your first mission is simple: Talk about their name.

THE TECHNIQUE : Ask a Question

The biggest barrier to remembering someone's name is hearing it. When we meet people, we're often distracted by our thoughts or what's happening around us. The name goes "in one ear and out the other."

No longer. As soon as you meet someone and they say their name, immediately repeat it, then ask a question about it. Using this technique accomplishes three essential tasks: 1) you prepare yourself to hear the name, 2) saying it out loud helps your mind start to remember it, and 3) asking a question cements it into your memory.

HOW TO DO IT >

Practice this technique ahead of time to make it easier to use successfully when it's important. Have a helper think of a name and introduce themselves. If you don't have someone to help, practice on your own by using any name you can think of. Continue practicing with your helper, changing roles so they get a chance to master this memory hack. Whether in a practice session or in a real-life scenario, follow these steps:

1   Since you know you're going to repeat the name and ask a question about it, your mind is already paying attention. As soon as they've said their name, repeat it in the form of a question. "Jeff?" They'll confirm that you have the name right.

2   Your mind has heard the name twice now—once from their mouth and once from your own. Your natural memory is doing what it knows to do: remember *important* information. Since it's heard the name twice, your memory realizes, "This is important."

3   Next, kick your memory into overdrive by asking a question related to the name. There are three methods to choose from:

   a]   Spell it: "How do you spell that?" or "Is that spelled . . . (spell the name)?"

   b]   "Is that short for . . . (the common full name)?"

   c]   "Oh, like . . . (mention a famous person with the same name)?"

Using the name "Jeff" in the example above, we have:

a]   "Is that spelled J-e-f-f or G-e-o-f-f?"

b]   "Is that short for Jeffrey?"

c]   "Oh, like Jeff Foxworthy?" or "Like DJ Jazzy Jeff?"

From now on your first conversation with someone new will be about their name. This technique makes meeting people and remembering their names simple, easy, and fun. To take this technique to the next level, read on to help other people remember your name.

[6] Teach People to Remember Your Name

YOU'RE LEARNING THESE incredible memory hacks and seeing how powerful they are. Your memory is improving, and people are starting to notice. You can use your newfound memory power to make the lives of others better. You'll use the technique from "Remember Names" on page 11 not only to help them remember your name but to introduce them to a technique they can use for the rest of their lives. You'll be paying it forward.

THE TECHNIQUE ⋮ Explain Your Name

This technique is similar to the previous one, but the roles are reversed. The people you meet are probably struggling to both hear and remember names—just like you used to. In fact, if you watch carefully, you may see the moment when a new acquaintance realizes they've already forgotten your name. You're going to spare them that fate. Mention that you'd like to not only remember their name but help them remember yours. To assist them, you'll spell your name, tell them what it's short for, and/or mention a famous person with the same name.

HOW TO DO IT >

1 The next time you meet a person, you'll immediately use one or more of the three questions from the previous technique to help your natural memory cement their name in your mind. For example: "Jenn? J-e-n-n, right? Is that short for Jennifer?" Then you introduce yourself and pay it forward.

2 Make sure you make eye contact and have their full attention. (If they are distracted by something happening around you, wait!) Say your name clearly and slowly. "Nice to meet you, Jenn. My name is . . ."

3 Choose one or two methods ahead of time to help them remember your name: 1) how it's spelled, 2) what your name is short for, and/or 3) the name of a famous person (or someone they already know). I'll use my name for this example:

> *"Nice to meet you, Jenn. My name is Brad. To help you remember that, I'll mention that Brad is short for Bradley, but I prefer Brad. Probably the best way to remember my name is to think of how much more exciting it would be if you were speaking with Brad Pitt instead of me! In fact, imagine Brad Pitt is my best friend, and he's standing right here next to me. I guarantee you'll remember the name Brad easier that way."*

You've helped your new acquaintance remember your name and started a fun conversation. They may not realize it, but you've saved them the embarrassment of not hearing or remembering your name. Way to go—not all heroes wear capes!

[7] Remember Where You Parked the Car

HAVE YOU EVER spent more time looking for your car in the parking lot than you did shopping? When I was young, my dad would say, "Remember where the car is . . . right next to that white one." Of course, cars come and go all the time, and every third car in the lot was white! Amazingly, though, we always knew where the car was because he drew our attention to not only the nearby white car but also to the overall location in the parking lot. A variation of my dad's technique will enable you to find your car quickly from now on.

THE TECHNIQUE • Focus Your Attention

The reason we lose our car in the parking lot is because we aren't paying attention. Later when we leave the store and can't find the car, it's less a matter of having forgotten than not taking a moment to remember in the first place. You will use your visualization and creativity skills to draw your attention to where you've parked using nearby objects in the area to orient yourself to the location. It takes less than a second, and it's an incredibly practical and easy skill to develop.

HOW TO DO IT

These are two similar techniques. The first one is more memorable because it uses the most creativity, but the second is a bit easier and quicker.

OPTION 1

1 Park the car.

2 As you exit, take a second to locate the nearest tree, light pole, sidewalk, sign, or other object that will be there when you return. Don't pick out another vehicle.

3 Imagine your car and the object interacting. The car could jump the curb and smash into the nearest storefront, have a sign fall on it, catch on fire and burn the nearby bushes, or roll backward and block the way for all the other cars.

4   Think about whether you will be able to see the imaginary commotion your car has made when you walk out of the store. This will link the direction of the car to the store.

5   As an added step, estimate the angle from the store's door to the car. Is it 5 degrees? 20? Are you straight in line with the entrance?

OPTION 2

1   Park the car.

2   Look toward the store or building. What is a memorable object in line with where your car is parked? Often there is a large sign with the name of the building or store. Pick the letter closest to the row you have parked in. If you're at BRAD'S BIG STORE and you're parked to the right of the entrance, the "R" in "store" might be in line with where you've parked. If you're parked along the street, estimate how many car lengths you are from an obvious point like a bus stop or the next intersection.

Try both variations of this technique to discover which one works best. Your mind will love you, and you'll never again have to walk around the parking lot clicking your key fob while listening for the *beep beep* of your car.

[8] Exercise Your Memory with Your Shopping List

"WHY SHOULD I remember my shopping list? I can just write it down or use my smart device to remind me." I promote memorizing your shopping list as an easy, no-pressure way to exercise your memory. By spending a few minutes using a fun memory technique, you'll exercise your memory, which will serve you in other, more important areas of your life.

This is one of the most fun techniques in the book. You'll connect each item on your shopping list using your creativity. Let your silly side come out, and remember the acronym CAST: add **C**olor, **A**ction, **S**ize, and **T**exture to your images. Turn lettuce into a heavy bowling ball and use it to knock down the huge carton of milk. Can you imagine rolling the lettuce from the produce aisle all the way to the milk cooler? Using this method, you will develop your ability to quickly think outside the box and prove how easy remembering anything can be.

I love this method because of how little commitment it takes. You can experiment with remembering 2 to 20 items on your shopping list; it's up to you. There is no need to fear because you'll still take your list with you to the store and use it as much or as little as you need. You may start small by thinking of the two or three most important items. Once you see success, you can add more and more until you have your list memorized every week.

HOW TO DO IT

1 Write out your shopping list.

2 Pick a few items to remember. I recommend selecting the most important ones.

3 Visualize the entrance to the store.

4 Use your imagination to picture your first item at the store entrance. Supersize it so it fills the space, spill it if it's liquid, unpackage it, or otherwise change it so it's memorable. Some examples are: Spill the spice all over the floor and imagine how it smells to walk into the store; a huge milk carton is leaking, filling the area with two feet of milk; or imagine having to eat through the giant loaf of bread to enter the store.

5 Connect your next item to the first in an interesting way. If you pictured the milk pool first, imagine using a huge loaf of bread to soak up the milk.

6 Continue adding to the crazy story using exaggerated visuals. This is no time to play it safe and picture a normal-size carton of milk sitting next to a loaf of bread. Go wild in your mind!

7 When you walk to the entrance of the store, visualize the story you created.

8 As you shop, the story should still be on your mind. If not, think of the entrance of the store and see the story again.

9 As you're standing in line, think of the funny things happening at the entrance of the store in your mind. Look in your cart to confirm you've picked them out.

As you improve, try adding more items each trip. Vary the location of the story so you don't confuse one trip's list with another.

TIP | HELP THE MIND REMEMBER WITH VIVID, CREATIVE IMAGES

Your creative images must be interesting and unusual, which the mind finds memorable. Exaggerate! Images should have CAST, including one or more of these: 1) Color, 2) Action, 3) Size, and 4) Texture.

---

[9] Remember Whether You Took Your Medicine

"DID I TAKE my medicine today? I think so . . . but maybe that was yesterday." Remembering the mundane is difficult because it happens repeatedly and is so automatic. But forgetting to take important medicine or accidentally taking it twice can have a huge impact. Using this easy method will ease your struggle to remember.

But here's a disclaimer: Taking medicine is serious business. This technique will help you remember *if* you took your medicine, but use an alarm to remind you *when* to take your medicine. Also make a written note of whether you've taken it or mark it on your calendar. Use your memory as a *backup* assistant. This is too important to rely solely on your memory.

THE TECHNIQUE ⋮ Notice and Make Noise

This technique links the mundane and easily forgotten with something more memorable. There is always something happening nearby to bring our attention to, whether it's the chirping of a bird outside our window, the weather, how we feel, or something on the radio or television. By bringing your awareness to the outside event and using your voice and a noise, you'll trigger your mind to remember the moment and what else you did, like taking your medicine. Later, if you question yourself, you'll immediately recall the words said and noises made to reassure yourself that you took your medicine.

There are two issues here. One is remembering to take the medicine on a schedule, which I addressed earlier. The other is remembering whether you've done it this time. Both are easy to forget. Here's how to use your mind to add an extra layer of protection to your medicine-taking routine.

HOW TO DO IT

1   When you take your scheduled medicine from now on, tell yourself out loud that you're doing it.

2   Add a comment that brings your attention to the moment. Things to note are the day and time, what is happening in or outside your home, the weather, and how you feel. For example, "I'm taking my morning medicine at 8 o'clock Tuesday. It's raining, and I feel tired, but there is a beautiful cardinal at the bird feeder."

3   Add a sound effect after you say it: Clap your hands, stomp your feet, whistle, click your tongue, or snap your fingers. Change these each time you take your medicine so you won't confuse this time with another.

This technique works for several reasons. First, you're bringing your attention to taking the medicine and no longer doing it without thought. Second, speaking about what is going on around you makes you take note of the moment, assisting your natural memory. Third, adding a noise is another reminder. Now you're noticing, making noise, and remembering.

[10] Never Forget a Face

MANY PEOPLE HAVE trouble remembering names but say, "I never forget a face!" There are some people, though, who have a harder time recognizing faces. In this case, their effort goes into remembering what people look like, then working to remember their names. This method will help you develop the habit of better noting people's facial features.

THE TECHNIQUE ⦂ Facial Scan

Faces have many common characteristics that you will start to note instead of just overlook. You'll start a facial scan, considering the larger details and progressing to the smaller ones until you feel you can close your eyes and picture their face. The thought process and overall goal is, "How could I describe this person's face so well that they'd be recognized by someone who has never met them?"

HOW TO DO IT

1   When you meet a person you want to remember, scan their head and face while speaking with them. Mentally name the shapes you see.

2   Start with the shape of their head. Is it round—with the length and width about the same? Oval? Oblong—which is longer and narrower than oval? Or is the face square, with the width of their jawline and forehead nearly the same? Less common face shapes are diamond, heart, and pear, which can be harder to note; many people focus on the first four.

3 Notice their eyes next. Are they hooded? Set close together or far apart? Wide? Narrow? Deep set?

4 What type of nose do they have? Turned up? Fleshy (think of Albert Einstein) or bumpy? Roman, like you might see on an ancient sculpture? Wide or narrow? Bulbous or sharp?

5 Finally, what type of mouth or lips do they have? Are they thin or thick? Narrow or wide? Round or pointy? Heart shaped? Is one lip narrower (upper?) than the other?

6 Quickly scan the person's face a second time while silently naming each part: "Round head, wide eyes, bumpy nose, narrow lips."

7 Look for any other features that stand out, like freckles, a mole, or small or large ears.

8 Briefly note their hairstyle and color, any makeup, and piercings, but keep in mind that these can change over time.

9 As soon as you're finished speaking with the person, mentally re-create their face while repeating to yourself the features you noted earlier.

10 Every night when you brush your teeth, review the faces of the people you met that day. Imagine them brushing their teeth next to you and see their faces in the bathroom mirror.

At first it may be difficult to both notice and describe the features, but with practice, it will become second nature. You will automatically scan the faces of people, and their images will be easier to remember.

TIP | THE TOOTHBRUSHING REVIEW

Dentists recommend that we brush our teeth twice a day for about two minutes each time. This is the perfect time to review what you want to remember. Whether it's the names of the people you met recently or the titles of books you read, take that time to review and remember.

[11] Recall Flight Numbers and Times

I WAS TRAVELING recently, and when I looked at the flight display board at the airport there were six flights scheduled going to my destination. Which was mine? Because I had used this technique to memorize my flight numbers, it was easy to find my flight, even with a change in the departure gate. Does remembering flight numbers, times, and gates sound difficult? It's not, and it's much easier than fumbling for a piece of paper or a smartphone to check the details every time.

Numbers seem hard to recall because they rarely mean anything to us. The solution is to both decide to remember and make the numbers meaningful. Use the MOST Method to creatively convert the numbers into:

- **M**oney
- **O**bjects
- **S**port scores
- **T**ime

HOW TO DO IT

Your Flight 8631 to Miami leaves at 9:35 a.m. To make those numbers easy to remember, you must make them more interesting.

1 **MONEY. Change the number into dollars and cents, and then think of what you could buy. What would you get if someone gave you an extra $86.31 or $8,631?**

2 **OBJECTS. Do the numbers remind you of any objects? Maybe you got your first car in 1986, and maybe you like Baskin-Robbins, which is famous for 31 flavors of ice cream.**

3 **SPORTS SCORES. Does the number inspire a comparison to a sport you enjoy? Could you run an 86:31 half marathon? Could you bench press 86 pounds? How would you feel if your favorite team won by a score of 86 to 31?**

4 **TIME. Flight 8631 doesn't relate to the time on a clock, but it can relate to the passage of time. Who do you**

know that's around 86 years old and 31 years old? Picture them interacting.

VARIATION FOR FLIGHT TIME

You can use the MOST Method for the time your flight leaves as well, or you might want to switch it up a little and use the Meals and Money Method. Here's how:

1 **What meal is the departure time closest to? If your flight is leaving at 9:35 a.m., it's closest to breakfast.**

2 **Now change the time to a dollar amount: "My flight is at 9:45 a.m., so I'll eat at the airport. I wonder what I can buy there for $9.45."**

TIP | GO TO THE RIGHT DEPARTURE GATE

How do you remember the letter/number combination of your departure gate? Easy: 1) Change the letter into a food starting with that gate letter: Gate A (apple), Gate B (banana), Gate C (cookie). 2) Imagine the gate number is the amount of food you have or how much it costs. For example, Gate A4: juggle four apples as you run to catch your flight. Gate C18? Imagine paying $18 for an airport cookie.

[12] Remember License Plates

DO YOU KNOW the license plate number on your car? Do you need to? One day you just might, and you'll want to avoid running outside to the driveway to check. Hotels often request your license plate number when you are checking in, and you'll need it in case your car is towed. And what about remembering the license plate number of the car that just caused an accident but left the scene of the crime? Luckily, committing license plate numbers to memory is easier than you might think.

Remember the letters in a license plate by changing them into interesting images using the Alphabet Image System. Alphabet images are made by connecting each letter of the alphabet to an item you can easily picture. I prefer food: apple, banana, cookie, donut, egg, French fries, etc. You're not limited to food, of course—use animals, people, or anything else you find memorable. Customize your list so you can easily picture each letter listed on the license plate. Then, you'll combine this technique with the MOST Method (see page 22).

HOW TO DO IT

1 Using the Alphabet Image System, convert each letter in your license plate to an image.

2 Make each of the numbers memorable using the MOST Method to change the numbers into money, objects, sports scores, or time.

3 Use your creativity to create a story about the plate number. Be sure to include action, exaggerate the size, and add color and texture to make the story as interesting as it can be. Here are a few examples:

- **3D1979**: Imagine three (3) **D**onuts that have been sitting around since 1979. Think of something specific that happened that year and how the donuts look after all this time.
- **EJU7909**: **E**ggs with **J**am and **U**rchin costs $79.09.
- **756WBR**: At almost 8 o'clock (756), a **W**atermelon fell off a **B**ridge onto a box of **R**aisins.
- **6TRJ244**: Imagine six (6) **TR**ucks covered in **J**am racing. The first two (2) are 4x4s (44).

[13] Remember Numbers Using the Simple System

THE MOST METHOD (see page 22) for remembering numbers has its limitations. Sometimes it can be difficult to convert numbers into images using money, objects, sports, or time. Since numbers make up so much of what people struggle to remember, we need another go-to method when MOST doesn't fit the bill. The Simple System is so easy that I recommend learning it yourself and then teaching it to your friends and family. Practice while shopping to get good at this system quickly.

There are two other number systems coming up, so don't dwell on any one too much until you read all four. Then you can decide which one is best for you.

THE TECHNIQUE ⁞ The Simple System

Unlike the MOST Method, the Simple System has predefined images already assigned to each number. Each number from 0 to 9 represents an image based on what it looks like or reminds you of. Here's an example, but you can customize the images to suit your imagination:

0	Donut or soccer ball
1	Baseball bat or candle
2	Pair of shoes

3	Tricycle
4	Stool with four legs or anything golf related ("Fore!")
5	Looks like a fishhook so picture a hook, fish, or bobber
6	Ant (six legs)
7	Looks like a boomerang
8	Octopus
9	Cat (nine lives)

For larger numbers, the images are combined. 98 could be a cat snatching an octopus out of an aquarium, for example. The system could be expanded, depending only on your creativity. Some are easy to fill in. For example:

10	A model who is a "perfect 10"
11	A speaker that "goes to 11"
16	First car
18	Tractor trailer (18 wheels)
21	Blackjack
64	The Beatles ("When I'm 64")

HOW TO DO IT

1   Create a list numbered 0 to 9. Then, using the examples as a guide, create your list of images.

2   To start using this system, practice with license plates as you drive or use any numbers you see throughout the day. The more you practice, the more second nature this will become and the more numbers you will remember. You can also do this at the store. For example:

> *Cookies cost $2.89. Imagine storing the cookies inside your shoes (2) as you go to the aquarium to feed the octopus (8). See the cat (9) on the edge of the aquarium hoping for a chance to grab the octopus.*

[14] Memorize the Month of Important Dates

PEOPLE ARE ALWAYS appreciative when their special days are
remembered—even more so if you know it's coming before being
reminded by social media or that relative who's always keeping track of
things! In this memory hack, you'll learn how to imagine each month so
you'll be able to make people feel good by remembering them on their
important dates. Keep in mind, you'll still need to link it to the actual
date, so this is just prep work.

THE TECHNIQUE : The Month Memorization System

The Month Memorization System relies on associating each month with
an image to help you better remember the months of important dates.
These images will be used in techniques further ahead in this book to
remember events, dates, and deadlines.

Although I'll include an example, you'll be considering what each
month reminds you of, often a holiday or an event that happens during
that month. Use whatever comes to mind first as it will probably be the
first idea that comes to mind next time, too. This makes remembering
the system even easier.

1 Think of each month of the year for a few moments. What holiday or image comes to mind? (Remember that not every month from November to April can be "snow" or "ice"!) Decide on a creative mental image for each month using my suggestions or your own ideas.

2 Add details to each image using CAST—a combination of **C**olor, **A**ction, exaggerated **S**ize, and **T**exture to make the images instantly come to mind later. When you think of a month from now on, the image should jump forward the same way you remember the icon of your favorite app or software program.

3 As you are brushing your teeth tonight, mentally review the months to confirm you have a solid image for each. If you can't instantly think of the month's image, create one and add a lot of CAST details to make it stick.

Here's an example:

Month	Holiday or Event	Other Ideas
January	New Year's Eve (Baby New Year or Father Time)	Icicles
February	Valentine's Day (Cupid, hearts, love)	Spouse, best friend
March	St. Patrick's Day (leprechaun)	Spring flowers (crocus)
April	April Fool's Day (fool) or Earth Day (planet)	Rain or umbrella
May	Cinco de Mayo (Mexican flag) or Mother's Day (Mom)	*Mayflower* (old-fashioned boat)
June	Father's Day (Dad)	Fireflies
July	Independence Day (fireworks or Uncle Sam)	Croquet
August	Summer (swimming pool)	Mosquitoes
September	Labor Day (barbecue)	Back to school (school bus)
October	Halloween (jack-o'-lantern)	"Oct"ave (piano)
November	Thanksgiving (turkey)	NO! (two-year-old child)
December	Christmas (Santa Claus) Hanukkah (menorah)	Snowman

[15] Remember Passport Numbers and Renewal Dates

PARTWAY THROUGH INTERNATIONAL flights, we're asked to fill out a customs and immigration form that includes our flight details (which we'll easily remember from the technique on page 22) and passport number. By knowing two different number memory techniques, you can memorize your passport number quickly, too.

With the Story Method, you'll never have to disturb your seatmates by digging through your carry-on bag to find your passport. As a bonus, people will think you're super smart because you can remember a nine-digit number!

THE TECHNIQUE : The Story Method

Most United States passports are nine digits. The technique for memorizing your passport number is to create a memorable story using the numbers. Give each number an image, using whatever idea jumps out at you first, such as a sports score or a dollar amount from the MOST Method (see page 22), an idea from the Simple System (see page 25), or something else that makes sense to you. You're creating a memorable story, so make it as real as any television show or movie you watched recently.

HOW TO DO IT

1   Find your passport (remembering where it is might be the hardest part of this technique!).

2   Change the numbers into images using the Simple System or the MOST Method.

3   Create an amusing story using the images from the number system.

4   Add the passport image or idea, so when you think of the passport you'll think of the rest of the images in the story.

5   Close your eyes and re-create the story or mental movie three times, adding more CAST details (**C**olor, **E**xaggerated **S**izes, **A**ction, **T**exture) each time.

6   Replay the movie or story tonight and tomorrow morning as you brush your teeth. The spaced repetition review will create an unforgettable memory.

7   Go above and beyond by learning the expiration month and year by adding to the original story. Convert the expiration month into an image using the Month Memorization System (see page 27) and connect it to the story along with the last two digits of the year, which you translate into images. Review these details to make sure they're vivid.

Here's an example:

Passport No. 477746628, Exp. June 2027

Imagine your basketball team losing 47–77 or your baseball team having a 47–77 record partway through the season. You sit on a stool (4), dejected, while two ants (6, 6) crawl up the legs before getting smashed by your shoes (2). You need a snack, so you pick them off the floor and eat ("ate"/8) them. Finally, you grab your passport to go visit your father (June, Father's Day) even though it's below freezing there—only 27 degrees.

[16] Instantly Remember Travel Directions to the Locals' Favorite Places

ASKING FOR DIRECTIONS is a great way to meet interesting people and discover the wonderful places locals know. Remembering those directions, though, can be tricky. After the second or third turn, our eyes glaze over. While we can usually rely on our smartphones or GPS devices, why not have the ability to recall directions as a "just in case"?

Instantly memorizing the name of a recommended place and the directions to get there doesn't take special effort. You will change the information into creative mental images and connect them together using the Story Method. First, you need a few pre-pictured images for directions—this is your personal Directions System. Here are some suggestions for converting these images:

- Left = sounds like "lift" or "heft," so picture lifting weights or barbells.
- Right = sounds like "fight," so imagine punching or boxing gloves. "Bite" is also a great image.
- North = alphabet word "nachos," or think of north meaning cold and icy.
- South = alphabet word "strawberry," or think of south meaning warmth and sunshine.
- East = alphabet word "egg."
- West = alphabet word "watermelon."

I often use left and right in practice, so be sure you have solid images for them.

HOW TO DO IT

While on vacation, you ask a local for a recommendation for a great restaurant. She says, "Try Dizzy Cow. Turn right at Lake Street, go two blocks to Broadway, and turn left. It's four blocks down on your right."

1 Change the name of the place into an image. Use your imagination and make it as silly as possible to make it memorable.

2 Convert the directions into images. Associate each image with the street name. Use Alphabet Images (see page 24) to convert the first letter of each street into an image if you can't quickly picture the street name. Don't be afraid to ask the person giving the directions to slow down or repeat them if you need time.

3 Connect each step together in a story chain or movie. Here's an example:

Picture a dizzy cow bumping into tables at the restaurant.

"Right at Lake Street."

Imagine finding boxing gloves (right = "fight") in a lake. Put them on your hands and wear them, dripping as you go.

"Go two blocks to Broadway and turn left."

Left ("lift") plus Broadway (picture an exaggerated, very broad street. Think of getting to that corner, bending down, and lifting the wide street).

"Four blocks down on your right."

In the Simple System (see page 25) four is the image of a stool. Picture sitting on a stool throwing punches (right = "fight") at the dizzy cow.

The effort you put into trying the technique will enable your natural memory to kick in and help. You may find yourself relying on a combination of the method—"Yes, it's right here, I remember the boxing gloves!"—and natural memory: "I don't remember exactly what the images were, but I remember it's a left here and four blocks down," because you are so focused you just . . . remember!

Practice with directions to your favorite restaurant, converting them into mental images as you go. You'll be ready the next time you're directed to a great place on vacation.

[17] Remember Your PINs

WE REMEMBER OUR primary ATM card personal identification number (PIN) because we use it often, but can you remember all your other PINs? How can remembering a four-digit number be so difficult? By creating a story about each debit or credit card, you can make remembering all the PINs easy. Never be stumped on the phone when asked by customer service what your security code is or be embarrassed at the store when you're asked to enter your PIN.

The Rhyme Time Number System, or simply Rhyme Time, converts numbers into images based on what each number rhymes with. Then you can easily create a fun story that includes the idea or image of each credit card or company that requires a PIN.

Personal identification numbers are usually short: Most are four to six digits, which is perfect for the Rhyme Time Number System. The key is to take the simple rhyming words and create silly stories—which are the kind that are memorable.

HOW TO DO IT

1 Gather your ATM and credit cards and the PIN associated with each. You may have to call your credit card company and ask them to issue you a new PIN if you don't have the information on hand.

2 For the numbers 0 to 9, think of a word that rhymes with the number and create an image of that word in your mind. Here's an example, which you can customize using words and images that work for you. Remember, all you're doing is rhyming the number with another word you can easily imagine.

Number	Rhyme
0	Hero (picture your favorite superhero)
1	Run or Fun (favorite activity or sport)
2	Chew (favorite food) or Shoe
3	Tree
4	Door
5	Hive (bees)
6	Sticks or Ticks
7	Heaven or Elven
8	Bait (worm) or Date (favorite romantic person)
9	Tine (fork) or Sign (stop, yield, etc.)

3   Picture your bank or financial institution. Use the colors of their logo or the physical location of the branch. Make this image interesting and exaggerated or you'll be unable to start a memorable story. Use this image as the first link in your story chain.

4   The second link is the image associated with the first digit of the PIN. Connect the two together using plenty of CAST (**C**olor, **A**ction, **S**ize, and **T**exture) details to make it interesting and memorable.

5   Continue translating each digit into an image and link it with a story.

6   Review the whole story, adding as much detail as possible. Here's an example:

Hometown Bank ATM: 5048

I picture my favorite teller at Hometown Bank on her way to work. Unfortunately, she is being pursued by bees (5). Luckily, her hero (0) Money Man swoops in wearing his suit made of dollar bills and helps her through the door (4) of the bank. She is so grateful she gives him some valuable worms (8) from the vault at the bank where they are stored.

7   Test yourself after 30 minutes and again tomorrow to cement the story and the numbers into your mind.

[18] Remember Credit Card Numbers with the Major System

A FEW TECHNIQUES ago you learned how to remember a nine-digit passport number. The same technique can be used for credit card numbers. If you need to remember many numbers, however, there is a better system than the Simple System and the MOST Method. Here, you'll learn the Major System, which is what most memory athletes use to remember long random numbers in minutes.

This robust system takes some extra work upfront but makes for quicker memorization going forward. Look it over and consider if the effort is worth the time involved to make the system your own. For most people, one of the other number systems is better.

THE TECHNIQUE ┊ The Major System

Don't get overwhelmed by this explanation—it's much easier to try than to read! The Major System is a mnemonic system first credited to Pierre Hérigone in the early 1600s. In it, each number is represented by one or more consonants. These are then used in combination with vowels (as well as *y*, *w*, and *h*) to create words that can be used to remember numbers. Confused yet? Hang in there—it's easy once you get started.

My version of the system is slightly different from others' and I've also simplified it for this book. Don't get stuck. Read through this once first to understand it, keeping in mind that this is a much bigger system than 99 percent of the readers of this book will ever need!

THE MODIFIED MAJOR SYSTEM EXPLAINED

Number	Letter/Sound	How to Remember
0	z	z for zero
1	t (can also use d)	t and d have one downstroke
2	n	n has two downstrokes
3	m	m has three downstrokes
4	r	Four ends in r
5	l	L is the roman numeral for 50
6	"sh" or "ch" sound	Shucks and church each has six letters
7	k or hard c sound	k looks like two 7s lying on their sides
8	f or ph (like phone)	A cursive f has two loops and looks like an 8; ph = f sound
9	9p or bP	p and b look like 9s flipped

IMAGES

Number	Images	Number	Images
0	zoo	7	hack (ax)
1	hat	8	hoof
2	hen	9	hop (rabbit) or pie
3	ham	10	t+z = toes
4	hair	11	t+t/d = toad
5	eel	23	n+m = Nome (Alaska) or gnome (note that pronunciation is important, not spelling!)
6	shoe or ash	24	n+r = Nero or winery

The best use of the Major System is remembering long numbers (or a lot of numbers in general). Since it's a two-digit system, instead of a single-digit system like the other ways of remembering numbers you've seen so far, it is quicker and more versatile. Overall, though, the method remains the same.

HOW TO DO IT

1 Familiarize yourself with the Major System, or realize it's more than you need and use one of the other number systems you've learned.

2 Translate each pair of numbers (or single digits) on your credit card into a suitable image.

3 Link each image together into a story.

4 Add the expiration date using the Month Memorization System (see page 27) and a number system of your choice.

5 Add to the story with the three- or four-digit security number.

6 Review a few times, adding details.

7 Test yourself after an hour. Translate the story back into numbers and look at your credit card to verify. Fix any problems by adding more CAST (Color, Action, Size, and Texture) details to your story.

Here's an example:

> **Mastercard**
>
> **5105223577532190**
>
> **Expiration November 2025**
>
> **Security Code 769**
>
> **51= l+t = light(bulb)**
>
> **05 = eel**
>
> **22 = n+n = nun**
>
> **35 = m+l = mail**
>
> **77 = c+k = cake**
>
> **53 = l+m = lamb**
>
> **21 = n+t = nut (I picture a squirrel)**
>
> **90 = p/b + z = bees**
>
> **November = Turkey**
>
> **2025 = n+l = nail**
>
> **769 = 7,6 = c+sh = cash + 9 = pie = money pie**
>
> ***Story:*** *I imagine using my credit card to buy a light bulb . . . which doesn't work. Shaking it, I notice there is an eel inside. A nun offers to return it for me (by mail) and gives me a cake before she leaves for the post office.*
>
> **Continue the story yourself or go try it with your credit card.**

This system takes some upfront effort, but it's worth it if you frequently need to recall your credit card number or other numbers. Try it with one credit card as a test of how far you've come.

[19] Remember What Your Family Says

KIDS OF A certain age can talk a lot. So can spouses, friends, siblings, and parents. How can we possibly remember all the things they say? If we frequently forget what they tell us, we're perceived as having bad memories at best and being unappreciative or uncaring at worst. Even though we call this "forgetting," the problem usually isn't with our memory; the problem is with our focus. We are sabotaging our natural memory ability because we aren't focusing on getting the information. If we don't get the information, we can't remember it later. But you can fix this now and improve your relationships.

THE TECHNIQUE What's Next, Um, and How Methods

There are three methods to help your mind pay attention when someone is talking to you:

1 The What's Next Method trains your mind to listen better by trying to guess what the speaker will say next.

2 The Um Method makes a game of counting the filler words that are used, like "um," "ahh," "well," and "like."

3 The How Method helps you focus by asking yourself, "How will I remember this tomorrow?"

HOW TO DO IT

Before you use a method to remember what someone is saying to you, follow these three general steps.

1 Make sure you have plenty of quality personal time: your commute, daily walk, exercise time, or the shower. You can space out, let your mind wander, or ponder your own ideas during those times. Your time with your family or friends is not the time to be scatterbrained.

2 If you need a minute to finish a thought or commit something to memory, ask for it. Then stop worrying about whatever is on your mind and focus on the other person.

3 Don't worry about what you will say next, the story you want to tell, or adding your own two cents. Just listen.

THE WHAT'S NEXT METHOD

1 As you are listening, ask yourself (not out loud) what the person might say next or what might happen next in their story. It could be guessing which words they'll use or the bigger picture of how the story ends. This sharpens your natural ability to listen by making a game out of paying attention.

2 Be careful not to get lost in your own version of their story. Allow yourself to be surprised if it isn't as you expected or proud that you guessed correctly.

THE UM METHOD

1 Listen carefully for the filler words we all use: "um," "ahh," "well," and "like."

2 Keep a rough count of each use without letting it interfere with listening to the story or keeping you from the discussion. (Don't be rude and point out people's filler words or their frequency.)

THE HOW METHOD

1 As someone is telling you something important (to them), ask yourself, "How will I remember this tomorrow?"

2 You can also ask yourself how you'd tell the story to someone else. This will help you pay better attention.

As with any activity, the more you practice, the better you'll get. These methods are a great start, but you may find that after a while you don't need them. You'll improve your ability to listen and your natural memory will take over to better recall what people say to you.

[20] Remember People's Details

I ONCE ASKED a friend of mine why she thought her restaurant was so successful. She remarked that she listened to every customer and tried to remember what was going on in their lives. When they returned, she was able to recall what they had mentioned, asking how their mom was, if they had found their kitten, or another personal detail. People flocked to the restaurant because they felt cared about. You can show the people in your life how much you care by remembering more details about them and what they are doing.

THE TECHNIQUE : The CARE Method

The CARE Method is an easy and effective way to remember details people mention about their lives. This method demonstrates how to be an effective, world-class, gold-medal listener. Each step helps your natural memory lock on to important things the person is saying, making them easy to recall later.

This process starts with a conversation, so you'll ask a question about the person based on what you know about them. Here are some examples:
- "What's new in your life?"
- "What have you been doing for fun lately?"
- "What have you been up to?"
- "How was your week/weekend/day/summer?"
- "Do you have any good books/movies/music/restaurants you'd recommend?"

As they answer, you will CARE: 1) **C**ommit, 2) Pay **A**ttention, 3) **R**epeat, and 4) **E**nvision.

HOW TO DO IT

1 **COMMIT.** Sometimes we don't bring our full attention to a conversation because we're thinking about what we will say next or we're just distracted. We may perceive the person as unimportant to us. From now on, though, the first step

in any conversation is to *commit* to being the best listener ever. Go for the gold medal in listening!

2 **PAY ATTENTION.** Listen not only to the words they are saying but to the emotions or thoughts behind the words. Ask yourself, "How do they feel about what they're saying?" or "Is there anything they're leaving out?" or another question that helps you pay attention. Let go of any desire to share comments or your own story. Focus completely on what the other person is saying.

3 **REPEAT.** Remember taking notes in school, picking out a few important words or phrases and adding them to your notebook so that later you can remember the rest of what the teacher said? This is similar.

   Listen for the essentials in the story and repeat them when it is appropriate. " . . . and then my dog got sick and I had to take her to the vet." Repeat: "Oh no, your dog got sick?" Repetition tells your mind that the information is important. It will automatically move that topic up a level of importance so you have a better chance of remembering it.

4 **ENVISION.** Take the words or phrases from above and translate them into exaggerated pictures. Picture her dog being sick. Even if you've never seen the dog, you can picture one and imagine her holding it with concern—adding emotion to the mental image will also help it stick in your mind.

   "Well, my son got his blue belt in karate, so we went to that last week." Repeat and envision: "Wow, a blue belt?" Picture a blue karate belt, but remember to exaggerate: Imagine all the kids in the karate class using the brand-new blue belt as a jump rope.

With only a little practice this method will become second nature. By following the CARE steps, you will start to remember more of what people tell you. When you speak with them next, your mind will automatically recall the mental images you supplied it with so you can ask, "Last time we spoke you mentioned your dog had been sick. How is she?" or "Hey, how's your son's karate going?" You'll show you care by remembering more details of people's lives.

[21] Remember Birthdays

YOU MIGHT THINK that with social media these days it's no longer important to remember birthdays, anniversaries, and other important dates. Wrong! Knowing someone's birthday before you're reminded or see it posted online makes them feel special. And what happens when they either aren't on social media or don't include their birthday in their profile? Remembering dates will show others how important they are to you. It will also make you look brilliant!

THE TECHNIQUE : Combine Systems

This technique uses a combination of methods you've already learned to visualize birth dates, but don't panic—it's easier than it seems! You'll use the Month Memorization System (see page 27) and your preferred number system—the MOST Method (see page 22), the Simple System (see page 25), the Major System (see page 35), or Rhyme Time (see page 33)—for the date and then combine them all using the Story Method (see page 29).

The beauty of this technique is that you can ease into it. Pick a few people to start with so you're not overwhelmed. Next, focus mainly on the month. Just being able to say, "Hey, isn't your birthday coming up sometime this month?" makes people feel wonderful!

HOW TO DO IT

1 Pick three people whose birthdays you would love to remember.

2 Ask when their birthdays are or look them up on social media or an old calendar.

3 Pick one person to start with and picture them. What do you see? What physical features make them stand out in your mind?

4 Think of the month of their birthday. Imagine what that month reminds you of, using your own experience or the Month Memorization System (see page 27).

5 Connect the image of your friend with the image of the month in a creative, exaggerated way.

6 Look at the date of their birthday. Using the number system of your choice, turn that date into a mental image.

7 Add that picture to the story you have so far.

8 Review the entire story from the first image (your friend) to the last (the date). Add details and exaggerate them to make it memorable.

9 Continue with other friends, making each mental story as silly and fun as possible. Here's an example:

> Abraham Lincoln: Focus on a mental picture of what he looked like.
>
> His birthday was February 12. February always reminds me of Cupid and love.
>
> Picture Abraham Lincoln with his long face, beard and tall hat playing Cupid, shooting a bow and heart-tipped arrow. Isn't that strange? Lincoln in my mind is always a very serious figure!
>
> The number 12 could be a candle (1) and shoes (2): In addition to the bow and arrow Lincoln has a burning candle on each shoe as he walks around finding people to help fall in love. Or from the Major System: 1 (t) + 2 (n) could be tine: he's invented a new bow that shoots an arrow with three tines (like a fork) with hearts on the end. Also, 12 makes me think of a dozen eggs that could be incorporated into the story.

Use your imagination to create an interesting story about Lincoln, and then move on to making your friends feel special by remembering their birthdays.

[22] Learn Odd Words for Games

MANY GAMES REWARD those who can remember odd words, especially two- and three-letter words or ones that start with "X." Once again, here's a memory hack to the rescue! If you are especially competitive, or play with those who are, this is the hack for you.

THE TECHNIQUE : Alphabet Images and Stories

This technique helps you remember out-of-the-ordinary words so you can recognize them among the letters in your tile rack. It doesn't help with the definitions, though, so don't use this technique on a vocabulary test! With a list of hard-to-remember words, it's a simple matter of using the Alphabet Images (see page 24) to transform the difficult to remember into the easy to remember—and help you win! Here are a few examples for the popular Scrabble game:

Word	Alphabet Images/Story
Aa	Ant crawling through an apple
Ab	Ants crawling on a banana
Ae	Ants scaring away an elephant
Ba	Banana attacking an ant colony
Da	Dog chasing an ant
Ef	Elephant throwing a frog
Gi	Giant with an iguana on his head
Xeric	Xylophone on the back of an elephant with a rat playing the xylophone with one hand and feeding an iguana a cake with the other.
Xerus	Xylophone on the back of an elephant with a rat using an urchin as a mallet to smash strawberries on it
Xi	Xylophone with ice cream melting all over it
Xis	Xylophone with ice cream melting and snails eating the ice cream
Xu	Xylophone protected by an umbrella
Xyst	Xylophone with yogurt smeared on it, strawberry chunks, and a turkey walking up and down the keys eating everything
Xysts	The plural of xyst: Picture two of the exact image from above.

1   Pick your favorite word game and find a list of playable words grouped by letter or number of letters online or in a book. Use this as your resource to create your list to memorize.

2   Using the sample table as a guide, jot down the words you want to remember and use Alphabet Images to create a memorable story for each word. (Creatively link each story to the table where you play, the board, etc. as your anchor.) Associate each story image with the game, or put all the images into the room where you play by connecting the images to the room's furniture.

3   Set aside a half hour to memorize as many words as you can for your favorite game. Then, next time you play, when you see you have an "X," for instance, you will start to think of the funny stories you've created, double-checking to see which other letters you have as you go. Then, add up those points!

[23] Remember to Remember

AS YOU IMPROVE your memory, there will be times when you want to remember something but you're too busy, sleepy, unfocused, or sick to make it stick in your mind. Maybe you're in the middle of a discussion, phone call, or otherwise don't have a piece of paper handy. You need a reminder to remember something later. Having mental hacks available for times like these eases the stress of worrying about forgetting something. Learn this simple method for when emergency situations pop up.

THE TECHNIQUE : The Obstacle Method

In the past, people used to tie string or yarn around a finger as a reminder for later. That's fallen out of fashion, but we can use other methods to remind ourselves that there's something we need to remember. The Obstacle Method is just that. It's simply a matter of placing an object (the obstacle) in an unusual place where you are sure to see it when you need to, such as before leaving for work. You can also change the orientation of a common object to make it noticeable. Seeing that object prompts you to remember to do something important.

The Obstacle Method is a simple, real-world way to remember things. It especially works great at night when you're sleepy and know that you need to remember something in the morning or to remember to do one thing before another.

HOW TO DO IT

1   When there is something important that you need to remember, such as remembering to take lunch with you before you leave in the morning, place an object in a place where you will be sure to see it the next morning (or change the orientation of an object).

2   When you see the object, immediately do the task that needs to be done. In this case, grab your lunch bag out of the refrigerator.

This sounds easy enough, doesn't it? But here are a few important tips:

- Do not hide the object in an unusual place! It must be out in the open and easily noticed when you wake up or before you leave. Location, location, location. For example, don't think, "I need to remember to take the spare keys tomorrow, so I'll put them in the freezer. I'm sure to remember that." You'll end up remembering that you have to take the spare key but won't be able to find it because there's nothing to associate the keys with the freezer. (Yes, this actually happened, but not to me!)
- If you change the orientation of an object, it must be obvious. Don't assume you're going to notice the upside-down magnet on the refrigerator and remember to take the leftover chili into work. Better to turn the kitchen chair upside down or put it on top of the kitchen table (or both).

- Don't put a shoe, book, or water cup somewhere it can be tripped on in the middle of the night or when you wake up. It won't do you any good to remember something in the ambulance on the way to the emergency room.

Here are a couple examples:

EXAMPLE 1

> *You're on your way out for a walk and you want to remember to move the clothes from the washer to the dryer when you return. Lean your doormat against the door as you go for your walk. As you try to enter the house, you'll notice the mat, which will remind you that you need to remember something. Your natural memory will figure out the rest.*

EXAMPLE 2

> *You're about to lie down in bed and remember you need to take the potluck dish to work in the morning. You don't want to find a pen to write a note or use a memory technique. Instead, grab a sock and place it in the middle of the bathroom floor, in the sink, or in the bathtub. In the morning, you'll see the sock in the unusual place and know there is something you need to remember. Of course other objects can be used if a sock isn't handy or if you normally have socks in unusual places!*

This hack is another example of helping your mind by offering it something unusual to latch onto.

[24] Easy Daily Memory Improvement

HERE ARE SEVERAL easy ways to make remembering better a daily practice. Best of all—they are fun! I recommend doing them on your daily commute, walk, or whenever you go out. These are also wonderful if you have kids or family members you would like to help with memory improvement.

A great way to improve your memory daily is to play memory games. You can do this on your own or with your family. There are three great options, all of which give you opportunities to use the memory techniques you've been learning throughout this book.

HOW TO DO IT

OPTION 1: I SPY

Remember the car game I Spy? The memory version is useful for frequently taken trips to or from school, the mall, or the store. Ask, "What are the main restaurants (or stores, signs, buildings, or any other noteworthy objects) between here and where we're going?"

Start with the first one and visualize the path: "Brad's Diner is the first restaurant; it's on the right side of the road. What's next?" Quiz your passengers (or yourself) on the color of the sign, the location of different items, what's in the window of the store, or anything that comes to mind. This is a great way to create Memory Palaces (see page 76)! Any journey can become a palace to fill with information.

OPTION 2: SECRET AGENT ESCAPE

This game is great to play on a medium-length trip or one that you take often. Use the Alphabet Image System (see page 24) to remember the license plates of cars traveling near you. One twist: Connect the license plate with the color, make, or model of the car so you can easily pick out specific vehicles near you.

Pretend to be a secret agent who is concerned with being followed. Are any cars following you? Do the same cars (with the exact license plates) travel the same roads with you from day to day? You'll know for sure because you've memorized the license plates.

The last game is an old favorite called Memory, which is used to improve both concentration and memory. Shuffle a deck of 52 playing cards and lay them out in rows. Each player takes turns flipping two cards up. If they match (two kings, for example) both cards are removed. Whoever has the most cards at the end wins.

If you're competitive, use a system to win. Mentally number each row and each column. As unmatched cards are turned over, think of three images—row location number, column location number, and card image (a king can be an image of king, an eight gets translated into an octopus if using the Simple System for numbers or a worm—"bait"—for Rhyme Time). This is a fun way to perfect the basics of a number system. There will be a small learning curve, but once you can quickly picture a funny story for 3-5-king (tree-hive-king), it will seem like you have special powers to remember exactly where each match is.

TIP | REVIEW THE DAY

Reviewing your day helps your mind by telling it what information is important to save. Focus on what you—and your family—need to remember by taking time each day to review. Ask your kids what happened in a class where they struggle. Don't take "Nuthin'!" as an answer. Get out the textbook or homework if necessary. A few easy questions will make a big difference. Instead of purposely sweeping it under the rug, their minds will make note that the material is important.

[25] Short-Term Memory Success

WHAT STARTED MY path to memory improvement was walking into rooms and realizing I couldn't remember why I had gone there. This terrified me. Why couldn't I remember something so simple?

I know others frequently experience this along with other short-term memory problems. Does your coworker ask you for something that you completely forget a minute later? Do you intend to bring a glass of water to your spouse only to show up in the other room without it? All issues like this are easily addressed with the 1-2-3 Method.

THE TECHNIQUE : The 1-2-3 Method

Have you ever played with a dog only to have her suddenly distracted by a squirrel? You can see the dog thinking, "Squirrel!" and she's off. That's how I picture our minds when we have short-term memory problems. We're happily doing our thing but easily get distracted by the next thing, and the next thing, and the next thing. If we're asked to do a task and get distracted, the task doesn't get done; that's our dog mind at work. To fix this, you will teach your mind to pay attention to what you want with a simple breathing exercise called the 1-2-3 Method.

This method will initially show how well or how poorly you focus. As you keep practicing, you will improve your ability to concentrate and be in the moment. This will eliminate being easily distracted. Your natural memory will finally have the help it needs to focus and will be able to help the way it's supposed to.

HOW TO DO IT

You'll need a device with a countdown timer for this method.

1   Sit upright with your feet on the floor. Avoid the comfortable couch or recliner. A stool, kitchen, or desk chair is great.

2   Set a timer for one minute.

3   Pick a sound in the room like the hum of a fan, the air conditioner, the refrigerator, traffic, birds, etc. You can also listen to quiet, non-distracting instrumental music.

4   With your eyes closed, focus on that sound for three breaths in and out through your nose, counting to yourself at the end of each exhalation (*one, two, three*).

5   After three breaths listening to the sound, switch your attention to an awareness of your breath going in and

out of your nose. Count at the end of each exhalation (*one, two, three*).

6   Switch your focus back to the sound for another three breaths.

7   Continue changing your focus after every three breaths until the timer goes off.

How did it go? Did your mind wander? Did you lose track of what you were supposed to be focusing on or what number breath you were on? Did you get sleepy? Stressed? These are all common problems and exactly why you're doing the exercise! If it wasn't very difficult, try it for two, five, or ten minutes. Do this exercise at least once a day and work up to at least five minutes. You're training your mind to focus, and you'll see improvement in only a few days.

PART

2

School and Personal Growth

Whether we're in school or not, learning is an important part of life. One of the best ways to keep our minds fit is to keep studying and learning as we age. This part of the book contains more essential tools and techniques for learning. Even if learning a particular subject holds no interest for you—like cellular mitosis or the first 30 digits of pi—please at least skim the explanation of the memory hack anyway. It will help your memory to practice the techniques. You may be surprised by how enjoyable it is and how much you learn.

[26] Remember by Hacking Your Motivation

SOMETIMES IN LIFE we have to study things we're less than enthusiastic about. Learning happens best when there is both need and desire, and we tend to struggle when we need to learn and remember information that doesn't really interest us. If we want to learn something but it's not immediately necessary to us—we think learning French would be fun but don't have a trip planned to France—we won't remember what we learn as well as if we were going to Paris in a month. But we can hack our motivation to focus our minds and naturally remember anything.

THE TECHNIQUE **The SPEAR Technique**

Think spearfishing—but for motivation. To help your mind remember, you'll hack your natural motivation for learning using:

1 **Support**

2 **Punitive measures**

3 **Envision**

4 **Advantages**

5 **Rewards**

In most cases, one or two of the strategies in this technique will serve your purpose. It's your job to discover which ones work best for you by trying them with your next learning endeavor.

HOW TO DO IT

SUPPORT

Work with another person to be there for each other when you're both lacking motivation.

1 Bookend study sessions by calling or texting before you start and after you finish. "I'm going to study for one hour

and really focus. I'll text you when I'm done to confirm I worked hard."

2   Hold each other accountable and pick each other up when needed.

I only suggest this strategy in extreme situations.

1   Decide whether you need motivation for a series of small things (homework or quizzes) or one large event (an exam or final class grade).

2   Pick a dollar amount that is painful to lose. For a series, each small amount should be painful, and the overall total should really hurt if you have to give it up.

3   Carefully choose a friend who can be supportive, no matter what.

4   Put the money in an envelope addressed to an organization you find abhorrent. It should be a cause you truly can't stand.

5   Give the envelope to your friend with instructions that, if you don't do what you've promised (study a certain amount, get a certain grade in the class), they will mail the envelope no matter what excuse you give or how much it pains you (and them).

6   Every time you're reluctant to study or do the work, think of your money supporting the horrible cause. You'll be amazed by how much you are motivated.

7   Follow through no matter what: Either do the work or make sure the money is mailed.

This strategy is a gentle approach and doesn't work as well for tough cases.

1   Set an alarm for five minutes. Use your imagination to picture how good it will feel to pass the test, get the grade

you want, etc. Picture yourself getting high fives from friends, doing a happy dance, or pleasing your family. Feel the pride and the relief of doing well. Add as many details and positive emotions as possible, even if you don't care that much.

2   Re-create that mental scene when you're procrastinating or avoiding your work. This will motivate you to get started.

This strategy works better than Envision if you're more logical than emotional.

1   List the advantages of learning the material. Write down everything that comes to mind, no matter how small.

2   List the disadvantages of not learning the material. How would not learning it be painful, inconvenient, or troublesome?

3   Review the lists any time you need motivation—recognize that it makes sense to just do the work even if you don't feel like it.

The reward must occur as close to the learning action as possible. Don't pick a reward that is days, weeks, or months away.

1   Select a small candy or other food treat that you love like M&Ms, almonds, or potato chips. (A jar full of quarters or a bell can be also be effective.) Put them just out of reach.

2   Pick a small part of the work to complete, like doing an assigned reading or answering a homework question. Receive *one* treat for every small step taken. Get out the book you have to read, eat an M&M. Read the first page, eat another M&M. Read the second page, have another one. (Or move quarters from the full jar to an empty one or ring the bell as your reward.)

3 You will quickly associate taking a learning action with your instant reward and start to desire the action so you can have your treat. *Do not reward yourself if you don't do the work.*

Believe it or not, you have an amazing memory. Think of all the things you remember on a daily basis. By using one or more of these strategies in the SPEAR technique, you will inspire yourself to do the work. Your natural memory will be much better once you're motivated to learn.

[27] Maximize Your Memory with Excellent Study Strategies

GOOD STUDY HABITS help your natural memory ability. Do you study consistently instead of trying to cram the material into your mind at the last minute? Do you know your goals for each subject or exam? Are you keeping your mind and body in the best possible shape for learning?

In this memory hack, you'll learn a few study habits to make sure you're motivated, focused, and working smarter to allow your memory to work at its maximum potential.

THE TECHNIQUE : Fine-Tune Your Learning Habits

The study strategies to maximize your memory are: 1) Motivate, 2) Focus, 3) Fuel, 4) Decrease Stress, and 5) Sleep. Ask yourself:

1 What's my motivation for learning this?

2 What is my attention span for this subject or study session? Knowing how long you can focus—which varies by topic—is important for successful studying.

3 Have I taken care of myself with healthy foods that support my brain? Eating a heavy meal before studying, not eating enough, or consuming unhealthy foods can lead to a poor study session.

4 How stressed am I right now? What can you quickly do to lower your stress level?

5 What is my sleep plan? The mind needs sleep to consolidate memory.

HOW TO DO IT >

1 Find your motivation. It may vary depending on the subject and your level of interest. Use the SPEAR Technique (see page 56) to inspire yourself to learn.

2 Work according to your attention span. I recommend 20-minute sprints followed by 5-minute breaks. I like the adage "Work expands to fill the time allotted it." When we study too long, we often pace ourselves to fill the time and work slower than if we had less time. How much can you learn in 20 minutes? Focus hard knowing you can relax for 5 minutes at the end of the sprint. Avoid multitasking. No TV, radio, music, texts, or other distractions during study sessions. It's less fun, yes, but it makes for better memory!

3 Plan your meals to make sure you have fueled your body with nutritious low-carbohydrate food and given yourself adequate time to digest before studying.

4 Stress is a huge hindrance to learning. Make sure you're exercising (in ways that are appropriate for your body and health) by doing yoga, meditating, or choosing other healthy ways to avoid stress.

5 Sleep acts as the glue that holds information in our minds. A short nap following learning helps in later recall. Getting enough sleep at night is essential to consolidate memory. If you aren't getting seven to nine hours of restful sleep each night (depending on your individual needs), experiment with going to sleep 30 minutes earlier than you have been. Do this for one week and see if there is an improvement in your natural ability to recall information.

Commit to studying with intention. Use these steps to help your mind learn the information successfully so you can recall it easily when it matters most.

[28] Retain More of What You Read

READING AND NOT being able to recall the material later is very frustrating. Why is it so hard to remember what we read? Part of the problem is focus. How often do we sit completely upright in a quiet location, with plenty of time and nothing else on our schedule than reading the book in front of us? With this hack you'll remember more of what you read, whether it's an exciting novel or a boring textbook.

THE TECHNIQUE ⦂ The FIT Method

There are three parts to the FIT Method:

1 **F**ocus

2 **I**nstruct

3 **T**ime Management

First, you'll take steps to focus your attention. Your natural memory is ready to remember what you read, but you need to help it by eliminating distractions. Next, you'll practice instructing someone else on what you've read. This helps your mind retrace the path of what it has just learned, making the information "stickier." Finally, you'll be managing your time wisely so you can review what you've learned, telling your mind that the material is important.

HOW TO DO IT >

1 **FOCUS. Turn off all media—unless playing instrumental music is helpful to block out distracting sounds. Don't multitask. Set an alarm so you can commit to the reading without worrying about the time. Think of at least two reasons why reading is the most important thing to do right now.**

2 **INSTRUCT.** Read with the intention that you will teach someone else the material. Highlight important passages or make notes (written or mental) to use when you teach. Stop at the end of each page or chapter (depending on the amount of detail). Look at a nearby chair, pet, or find a friend and pretend you're the instructor. Teach them the material. Yes, *out loud—it will help your memory*. Refer to your notes as little as possible. If you do have to look, read them to yourself, pause, then look at the "student" and instruct them from your memory, *not* by reading the notes. You're making your mind work at recall, which is the important part. Simply reading your notes or the highlighted sections of the book isn't as effective.

3 **TIME MANAGEMENT.** Don't spend your whole session reading—or even reading and then teaching. Allow time to mentally review the important points from each page or chapter. Look at your notes or the pages briefly, then close your eyes and think about each detail. This mental review should be at least the third time your mind focuses on the words and concepts. It will prioritize the retention of important information, and the way we communicate importance to our natural memory is by reviewing.

[29] Remember Entire Books

IMAGINE BEING ABLE to recall an entire textbook or any other book. Impossible? Not at all. You can remember entire movies—why not books? What's different between the two? Movies are interesting and visual, but most textbooks aren't. We'll change that by making textbooks so fascinating and easy to picture that you'll be able to close your eyes and see any major or minor point you choose. Does this take time and effort? Definitely. But the approach is much different from studying—it's creative and fun. And, in my experience, it takes less time than traditional note-taking. Plus, it yields better short- and long-term memory results.

Mind Mapping is a technique many have heard of, but few have tried. It turns words, concepts, and facts into pictures. The mind loves images and finds them incredibly easy to recall. By converting the important parts of each chapter into a large drawing, the mind can visualize the layout of the information. And according to a study by researchers from the University of Waterloo, the act of drawing aids the memory better than writing out information.

Are you a horrible artist? Don't worry. Mind Mapping relies less on artistic ability and more on using colors, shapes, and connecting lines to make information memorable.

HOW TO DO IT

1   Start with the book you want to remember (or just one chapter of a book for practice). Write the title in the center of a large piece of paper held horizontally (longer side to side). Don't use a digital mind mapping app or program. This technique works best by putting pen to paper. The act of drawing shapes and adding lines, boxes, and circles is important to remembering.

2   The main ideas (often chapters) are linked to the title using different colors, thicknesses of lines, and a variety of shapes. Convert any ideas you can into sketches, even if they are crude stick figures. Continue with each important point that you want to remember later. If the book is filled with details to remember, consider creating a mind map for each chapter.

3   When you're finished, review your mind map(s). Study the connections, the shapes, and the lines while you review the information. Test yourself. Close your eyes and see where the data is on the page, what color it is, what shape surrounds it, or how it's connected to the rest of the information.

4   To learn more about Mind Mapping, see the Further Reading section on page 166 for the titles of two great books on this powerful tool, or search online for examples of memorable mind maps.

[30] Prepare Your Mind for Tests

YOU MAY REMEMBER the three essential memory steps (FAR) from earlier in this book: 1) **F**ocus on the information, 2) **A**rrange the material in the mind, and 3) **R**etrieve it when you need it. If you don't remember, see page 4.

Many people struggle most with the third step (retrieving the information) when taking tests because they get stressed. They haven't forgotten the material; after the test, the memories often come flooding back. Remembering too late, however, doesn't help you pass tests!

Using the techniques in this book to focus and arrange the material will go a long way toward solving the problem. But there are other techniques for keeping your cool and recalling what you've already learned. The goal is to be able to access the information when it can most benefit us, not long after we need it.

THE TECHNIQUE • Ring Your BELL

It can be natural to feel stress when taking tests because they are important. We want to do well; we're being tested! We need to calm down so that our minds can recall what we've worked hard to learn. Like the SPEAR Technique on page 56, these stress hacks will prepare your mind for tests at school, work, or life. To relieve stress, just ring your BELL:

1 **Breathe**

2 **Envision**

3 **Laugh**

4 **Later**

Do some or all of the following BELL steps as needed early in the day, and then do them again just before test-taking time. Your stress levels will decrease and your mind will sharpen, enabling you to better recall everything you worked so hard to learn.

BREATHE

Practice one to five minutes of diaphragm breathing.

1   Close your eyes and sit up straight.

2   Exhale completely through your nose, focusing on getting all the air out of your lungs and your diaphragm (stomach) area.

3   Inhale through your nose, filling your diaphragm first, then your lower lung area, and finally your upper lung area. Aim to do this with a slow count of four.

4   Exhale completely from the top of your lungs to your lower lungs and finally your diaphragm, aiming for a count of eight (or double the length of your inhalation).

5   Relax your shoulders and the rest of your body as you breathe. Release any stress in your body and mind along with your breath.

ENVISION

Spend one minute envisioning success on your test.

1   Picture the room or location where you will be taking the test.

2   In your mind's eye, place yourself in the room.

3   See yourself being relaxed and happy, even if it seems impossible at first. Use your creativity to picture this.

4   Imagine yourself confident, successfully turning in your paper and being satisfied with the results.

LAUGH

Think of a funny thing that happened recently or something you saw on TV that made you laugh. Make an effort to at least smile—or even laugh out loud.

LATER

Think of all the other tests you've taken. Whether you did well or not, there was always a "later." Think of what you'll do after this next test. Life will go on. You'll go to the next class, to work, or otherwise continue living your life.

    Thinking of "later" takes away much of the stress and fear. Often, our minds make the test the biggest thing in our lives, so this puts it in perspective.

[31] Remember How to Spell Any Word

THESE DAYS IT can seem that spelling isn't important since we do most of our writing on devices. Autocorrect and spell check place red lines underneath misspelled words, and the correct spelling is a click away. But spelling well isn't difficult. We usually know how to spell most of the word but struggle with one or two letters. Are there two *c*'s or one? One *s* or two? An *a* or an *e*?

    All we need to do is remember these problem areas, which is very easy to do with the Link Method.

The Link Method uses your imagination to picture two images, one for the word and one for the commonly misspelled part. By combining the two images into a memorable, silly story and adding details, you'll never again forget how to spell difficult words.

HOW TO DO IT

1   Find the correct spelling of a word.

2   Translate the word into a picture. Don't picture how the *letters* look, picture the meaning of the word.

3   Note which part of the word you misspell. Change that part into a picture.

4   Link the two pictures together to form an amusing story filled with detail.

Here are three examples:

Broccoli

Picture broccoli, all green and delicious (right?). Supersize it. Make the head of the broccoli six feet tall. Most people wonder if it's spelled with one c or two. Change the c into a picture: it could stand for cowboy, clown, cake, or cookie. Imagine two of them, since you need to remember there are two c's. Link the two cowboys with the huge broccoli in an amusing story: Two cowboys out West sitting next to the fire, roasting a huge head of broccoli on a spit.

Appearance

Picture a magician making something appear. Many people forget that it's ance, not ence. Translate a into a picture: ant, apple, aunt. Link the magician and the ant, apple, or aunt together. The magician you hired for the kids' birthday party makes a mistake, and a red fire ant appears instead of a cute bunny. The ant escapes and . . .

Calendar

Picture a calendar with full color pictures of— whatever is coming next. It's ar at the end, not er. Picture ar: How about a pirate? (You just said, "Arrrrrr" in your head, didn't you?) Link the calendar and the pirate.

Spending five seconds using this method ensures you'll never forget how to spell words that used to trouble you. Feel the pride that comes from becoming a person who spells well all the time.

TIP | YOUR MEMORY DETECTIVE

We each have a "memory detective" working in our minds that wants to help "solve the case," just like a detective on TV. What do the TV detectives have that your memory detective needs? More clues! Providing your memory detective with the clues it needs will make remembering everything easier. The clues are silly mental images created when we translate boring (forgettable) information into interesting (memorable) images.

[32] Keep Track of Commonly Mixed-Up Words

SPELL CHECK DOESN'T catch mix-ups like "you're" and "your" and "their" and "there." But confusing these words can make us look unintelligent. They're easy mistakes to make, especially when we're busy or in a hurry, like when we're posting on the Internet.

With a little focus and this technique, though, you'll be a master of memes and a scion of social media.

THE TECHNIQUE : Translate Words into Images

This technique is like the Link Method on page 67. You'll find the differences in the words and then translate those differences into pictures to recall the correct word usage and spelling. I'll be doing most of the heavy lifting in the following section by giving you the information and how to remember it. But using my examples, you'll be able to do it yourself as needed.

HOW TO DO IT

1 Make sure you understand the correct usage or definitions of the commonly confused words.

2 Think of the first word and picture its meaning.

3 Note what makes it different from the similar-sounding word. Often it's the spelling or an apostrophe.

4 Create an exaggerated picture or story that creatively combines the meaning and the difference in spelling using an Alphabet Image (see page 24).

5 Repeat the steps for the other word.

6 Immediately quiz yourself and add details to the images, as needed, to cement them in your mind.

Here are some examples of commonly confused words:

FEET/FEAT

1 Picture the meaning. "Feet" are at the ends of legs. Add exaggerated details to your mental image.

2 What makes "feet" different from "feat"? Two *e*'s instead of *ea*.

3 Picture two feet being stepped on by two elephants (*e* = elephant).

4 "Feat" is an achievement. It has *ea* plus a *t*, so imagine eating so much it's a huge accomplishment.

TO/TWO/TOO

1   "To" is used for motion in a direction or to express location.

2   It has only one *o* (and no *w*).

3   Imagine giving something (like an orange) to someone or taking it to a place. Don't just hope you'll remember the definition and example. Take five seconds to visualize a story.

4   "Two" is a number. The spelling difference is *wo*—picture two of something that starts with *wo* (like wood). Add details by building two of something out of the wood (skis because they go on two feet).

5   "Too" means "also" or an excessive amount. Picture something you wouldn't want to eat too much of, like an onion and okra salad. (Translating each of the *o*'s into a picture.)

YOUR/YOU'RE

1   "Your" is possessive; it shows ownership.

2   Picture "your" by thinking of a friend's pet, *r* like a rat or rhino (Do not picture a word that starts with *re*, as we will use *re* to imagine "you're"!). Ask the friend a lot of questions about their pet.

3   "You're" is a contraction of "you are." *R* = raisin, *e* = elephant. Imagine telling your friend, "You're going to wear this raisin costume and ride an elephant. It'll be fun!"

4   Remember, it just has to remind you or cue the memory. It's a hint; your memory detective will fill in the blanks (like the apostrophe).

ITS/IT'S

1   *Its* means possession, belonging to. Imagine your own arm p*its*.

2   *It's* is a contraction of "it is." Imagine a flying apostrophe chopping off the second *i* in "it is." The *s* moves closer to the *t* to be safe.

LOSE/LOOSE

1 "Lose" is for when you can't find something—like the second *o* in "loose"!

2 "Loose" is when something isn't tight or is set free. Imagine opening a gate so a g*oose* (because it rhymes with "loose") can be free of its cage.

HERE/HEAR

1 This is an example where it's necessary to commit only one word to memory. "Hear" is when you perceive a sound. Remember that you "hear" with your ear.

These examples show how to become smarter using your memory and creativity. Apply this concept to your own frequently mixed-up words. Take five seconds to forever remember the ~~wright write~~ *correct* way to use any word.

[33] Learn to Speak Foreign Languages

LEARNING A FOREIGN language at any age is a true test for the mind because it's all about memory. Fortunately, memory techniques make learning languages so much easier than rote memorization. Think of memory techniques as a bridge between not knowing a word at all and being so familiar with it that it pops into your mind without any effort.

Memory techniques are a means to an end, with the goal of thinking in the language without having to search your mind for the word. Using the method described here makes the language easier and faster to learn, and possibly even more fun.

THE TECHNIQUE ⦙ **The CAR Method**

Rote memorization to learn a language is possible, but it's like walking: slow. This method is like driving a car: much faster and easier. My goal here is not to teach you any particular language but to show you how to use the CAR Method to help your mind learn more words faster. You will use your imagination to:

1 **C**onvert each word (in English and the foreign language) into an image.

2 **A**ssociate them with each other in a fun way to make remembering them easier.

3 **R**epeat the process with more details, making the connection stronger.

HOW TO DO IT

1 Start with the English word. Convert it to an image. Remember to make the image interesting with CAST (**C**olor, **A**ction, exaggerated **S**ize, and **T**exture).

2 Correctly pronounce the foreign word. Convert it into an image based on what it *sounds like*, not its spelling. If necessary, break the word into syllables and convert them to images.

3 Associate the images together in a silly or strange way.

4 Repeat the association, adding more details to make the resulting image or story more interesting.

Here are three examples:

SPANISH: cat = *gato*

1 Convert *cat* into an interesting picture: a new breed with green shaggy fur.

2 Convert "gah-toe" into a picture. To me it sounds a little like "got" and "toe."

3 Associate the two images. Picture the green furry cat pouncing on your big toe, using its claws to hold on. The cat has "got" your "toe."

4 Repeat and add more details: Picture the cat using its sandpaper-like tongue to lick your toe. Imagine how that would feel.

JAPANESE: cat = *neko*

1 Convert *cat* into a picture like in the first example.

2 Convert "neck-oh" into a picture. Imagine your neck.

3 Associate the images: the green cat leaps up, lands on your neck, and starts licking it.

4 Repeat, adding details. You exclaim, "Oh, the cat is licking my neck!"

FRENCH: week = *semaine*

Variation: Start with the foreign word.

1 Convert "sem-enn" into a picture. It's a French accent version of "cement" without the *t* at the end. Picture a cement driveway or sidewalk near your home.

2 Convert "week" into a picture. That's a little tough, isn't it? Don't worry. If you can't quite picture a word (in either language), move to the next step.

3 Associate and get creative: Your cemen(t) driveway of fresh sloppy concrete takes a week to dry. Even though you're not exactly picturing a "week" your mind will make the connection. Your memory detective is very good at solving the case with a few clues.

4 Repeat with more detail. Picture how you feel when the neighbor's kids step on the cement on day six, leaving footprints that will last forever.

You don't need to use the CAR Method for every single word. Use it only for the words that you don't recall by reading, doing homework, and practicing aloud. If you hear the words pronounced slowly and correctly, you can creatively convert them. Don't worry about being exact or literal. Use your creativity and what each word reminds you of to speed up your ability to learn any language.

[34] Spell Words in Foreign Languages

THE CAR METHOD (see page 71) showed you how to remember spoken foreign languages. The Commit 2 Creativity (C2C) Method will help you spell these words correctly as well. Most people put a priority on speaking a foreign language, but knowing how to spell the words is also helpful. The problem is remembering how to say the word is often completely different from remembering how the word is spelled. Accessing your creativity will make spelling easy.

THE TECHNIQUE : The C2C Method

Many words can be sounded out and easily spelled. Studying a language and doing exercises will allow you to keep the spelling of them in your mind. But for words that are tricky or otherwise aren't easily remembered, you'll Commit 2 Creativity. This is the Link Method (see page 67) with a twist for remembering the word in English and the foreign language.

You will look at the words and think of creative ways to convert each letter, syllable, suffix, or hard-to-remember part into an image. Then you'll connect that to the image of the word. It's all about creativity, asking yourself, "How can I creatively transform this into an image?"

HOW TO DO IT >

1 Look at the word that is difficult to spell. Which part is hard to remember?

2 Creatively convert each letter or syllable into an image.

3 Connect that image to the foreign word and add the image of what it means.

Here are three examples:

EXAMPLE 1: Use your creativity to remember the whole word.

Semaine *("week" in French)*

Memorizing the spelling is easier if you've already learned the meaning of the word. If

*you've taken time to form a mental story, it's
even easier:*

*The wet concrete ("cemen") in front of the
house is happening all over southeast Maine
(s-e-maine).*

EXAMPLE 2: Remember which words have which suffix.

*This is common in many foreign languages, but
French has many words that end in -en, -enne,
and -aine. Commit 2 Creativity by associating
an image with each suffix and add that image
to the mix when you remember the meaning of
the word.*

*-en: Associate an English muffin, a penguin, or an
endangered animal of your choice to the words
that end in -en.*

*-enne: Connect an image of two nuns each riding
an elephant with any word that ends in -enne.*

*-aine: Link romaine lettuce or an ant in an egg to
words that end in -aine.*

**EXAMPLE 3: Use C2C to create your own system to remember
when to use each of the German spellings for the word "the."**

*"Der" sounds a bit like "dare." Associate a dare
with your image of the word, like* der honig *(the
honey). Can you think of a strange honey dare?*

*"Die" sounds like "dee" but is as easy to remember
as "die." Imagine* die ahnugh *(the idea) being so
bad it kills you.*

*What does "Das" sound like to you? How
could you imagine and associate it with the
correct words?*

[35] Remember What You Hear or Think About While Busy

A COMMON MEMORY frustration is not being able to remember something while engaged in a task like driving, exercising, or cooking. Wouldn't it be nice to listen to the radio on the way to work and remember the name of the book that was mentioned or the song that was played? Or to remember the task you need to complete after you are finished making dinner?

In these situations, we don't have to write down reminders or tell our smart devices to remember for us. We can make mental notes to recall later and store them in our Memory Palace.

THE TECHNIQUE : Memory Palace

A bit of easy prep work is required for this technique, but it's worth every second. Remembering anything requires us to arrange new information in our minds in ways we can easily access later. One way to accomplish this is to store it in a Memory Palace.

A Memory Palace is simply a well-known location that you can easily picture in your mind. Your current home or favorite store can be Memory Palaces, among others. In this case, you'll use a vehicle as your Memory Palace to save information for later.

There are two parts to this technique: creating a Memory Palace for later and then placing the information you want to remember in the location.

HOW TO DO IT

PART 1: CREATE A MEMORY PALACE

1 Imagine your favorite vehicle. Use a vehicle you have memories of, whether it's your family sedan or a subway car from your commute—whatever you can easily picture in your mind.

2 Create three areas in the vehicle that are distinct. If you're imagining a car, I suggest the front passenger's seat, rear driver's-side seat, and rear passenger's-side seat.

That's it! Good job, you've just created your first Memory Palace. You'll use it as a mental filing cabinet to store information to remember for a few days. Now let's see the tool in action. While listening to the radio you hear the title of a book you want to remember to buy: *Mastering Memory* by Brad Zupp.

PART 2: PUT THE REMINDER IN YOUR MEMORY PALACE

1   Convert the title or the author's name into an image. In this example, to picture Brad you might think of the actors Brad Pitt or Bradley Cooper. Either way, visualize the information in as much detail as you can quickly. Imagine Brad Pitt in the first location of your Memory Palace: the front passenger's seat. To add my last name, imagine a zebra starting to float *up* and, of course, imagine the zebra sitting in the front seat on Brad Pitt's or Bradley Cooper's lap.

2   When you have a second item to remember, repeat this process: Translate it into a picture and imagine it interacting with your next Memory Palace location. You want to ask a friend to lunch? Picture her eating in the backseat of your car. Add details like how much of a mess she's making.

3   When you hear a third thing to remember, again repeat the process. If you find yourself needing more room to store memories, add locations in your palace like the hood, roof, and trunk of the car.

4   Mentally review your Memory Palace each morning and night to see what's there. Take action when needed with what you find: buying the book you wanted, finding the song you heard and remembered, or calling the person you thought of. The location's memories fade quickly if they aren't reviewed, so they should be "cleared" for use each day.

[36] Remember a Series of Items Like the Bill of Rights

WE OFTEN NEED to remember the items in a series, like the proper steps to take, a list, a safety checklist, a way to figure out a math problem, or even the Bill of Rights. Whatever it is, memorizing steps in a series is often difficult. The Chain Method will make recalling any process a breeze.

THE TECHNIQUE ⋮ The Chain Method

Without even realizing it, you've already used the Chain Method when you memorized your passport number, credit card number, or PIN. You translated the steps of the process into images. They are connected like links in a chain, one leading to the next. In this way, you can connect an unlimited number of ideas or steps. The key is creating vivid images for each link and for each connection. In this version, you'll practice with words and concepts instead of numbers. I also introduce a slight variation that many people find easier than the original Chain Method used for numbers.

HOW TO DO IT ⟩

1 Translate the title of the process or series into an image. This will be the anchor that the chain is connected to.

2 Translate the first step into an image. Make the image exaggerated and interesting. If possible, find a person or character that can star in the story or movie. Add the character to each scene to make the story easier to imagine.

3   Translate the next step into an image and connect the first and second steps together in a creative way.

4   Take the third step, imagine it, then connect it to the second.

5   Continue visualizing and connecting each step in the process.

Here's an example: the Bill of Rights. I simplified the Bill of Rights for this example; it's helpful to select the key points prior to visualizing your chain.

Create an anchor image for the Bill of Rights: a famous person named Bill knowing his rights.

1   **FREEDOM OF RELIGION, SPEECH, PRESS, ASSEMBLY, THE RIGHT TO PETITION.** Create an image involving religion (a cross, Star of David, etc.) with speech, press, assembly, and petition. I imagine a cross behind a man giving a speech to a room of reporters who have assembled to pet their dogs (which is easier for me to visualize than petition). To connect it to the anchor (Bill), I see Bill Gates, Bill Nye, or Bill Murray giving the speech.

2   **THE RIGHT TO BEAR ARMS.** Imagine a bear with guns or a bear with muscular arms. Connect it to the previous link by seeing the bear walk into the room of reporters.

3   **HOUSING SOLDIERS.** Picture the bear at home when soldiers come to the house and want to stay there.

4   **SEARCHES AND SEIZURE.** The soldiers search the bear's house and seize the honey they find.

5   **RIGHTS OF THE ACCUSED.** The bear protests that he's never seen that honey before; he's innocent until proven guilty.

6   **FAIR AND SPEEDY TRIALS.** The bear goes to the state fair (Ferris wheel, etc.), where he stands trial.

7   **JURY TRIAL.** Various animals of the forest file in to be the jury.

8 BAIL, PUNISHMENT, FINES. The jury allows him to go free on bail.

9 OTHER RIGHTS ("DENY OR DISPARAGE"). Out on bail, the bear stands alone in the woods, careful to keep to himself and not *dis* any other animals.

10 UNDELEGATED POWERS. The bear delegates magical bear powers to the animals that live in different states.

To recall which right is associated with which number, simply imagine the story, counting the links until you reach the number you need to know.

Does this cover the whole Bill of Rights? Not even close. In memorizing a list or process, you will naturally have to cut much out. The Chain Method provides a reminder for the information you already have and gives your memory detective clues to solve the case.

[37] Remember the Five Phases of Mitosis

THE CHAIN METHOD (see page 78) and your imagination will make it easy to remember the phases of mitosis (the process that takes place in the nucleus of a dividing cell). If you struggle to remember not only the phases but also the details, though, you may need to use a Memory Palace (see page 76). I'll cover both in this section, so choose the one that works best for you. And, hey, if you don't need to know this, try the technique anyway and impress someone with your newfound scientific knowledge.

THE TECHNIQUE : The Chain Method or Memory Palace

You'll convert each phase to a mental image and attach it to the next one in the chain just like you did for the Bill of Rights (see page 79). To remember more details, like centrioles and what happens during each stage, you should use a Memory Palace. Pick a room you know well in your home (or the science classroom at school) and create a Memory Palace by imagining each wall and corner as a location for storing information. Then all you have to do is fill each location with details, starting with the names of the phase.

HOW TO DO IT >

PROPHASE • METAPHASE • ANAPHASE
TELOPHASE • INTERPHASE

To form the creative images for the Chain Method or Memory Palace, use your creativity to break down the words. What do they remind you of?

CHAIN METHOD

1 **PRO.** Think of your favorite pro sports team or player.

2 **META.** Think of the New York Mets (Meta). Connect your sports player or team with the Mets.

3 **ANA.** Think of an apple or an ant. Use whatever works best in your imagination to connect to the previous link (the Mets).

4 **TELO.** Picture a telephone. Since we usually use the word "phone" these days, picture an old-fashioned telephone to make it easier to remember "telo." Connect "telo" to the apple or ant from the previous link in the chain.

5 **INTER.** Think of an intern, a doctor who is in training, but if that doesn't work in your mind, use an image from the movie *Interstellar*.

Here's an example:

> *I imagine that Tiger Woods (pro golfer) walks into the New York Mets stadium. He picks up an apple that is on home plate. A bat boy brings him an old-fashioned telephone. He hangs up and hits a baseball so far that a man in space catches it.*

To remember all the details and parts of each phase, use a Memory Palace such as your science classroom. It helps to start with the phases, centrioles, DNA, etc., as illustrated images. You should be able to picture what the DNA condensing and centrioles moving look like— but magnified so large you can see it happening in the air, like fish in an aquarium.

Here's an example:

> *Picture Tiger Woods* (prophase) *in your science room. He is doing division on the whiteboard (in the prophase, a cell gets the idea that it's time to divide). Tiger duplicates the image of DNA in two places on the board; he's getting everything ready (imagine pennies for* centrioles) *for the process of mitotic division—picture your* (my) *baby* (tot) *spitting out food* (ick!).

> *In the corner near the board, you can picture the New York Mets* (metaphase). *Imagine all that happens in this phase (refer to your textbook) by changing them into pictures and seeing them happen in that area of the room.*

This memory hack makes the phases easier to remember, but you still need to learn the material. It's a tool, not a shortcut! Experiment and see how well it works.

[38] Remember the Digits of Pi

PEOPLE ARE AMAZED when I recite digits of pi. Of course these days even remembering phone numbers seems difficult, but pi is no harder than that. Want to impress people (in a nerdy way)? Memorize 30 digits of pi. It's easier than you think using the concepts already presented in the book.

After what you've learned so far this one is pretty easy. You can make this a game by thinking of it like a secret code. You will be using your favorite method for translating numbers into images: The MOST Method (page 22), Simple System (page 25), Major System (page 35), or Rhyme Time (page 33). If you haven't picked your favorite one, now is the time.

In case you don't already have them memorized, which I bet you don't if you're reading this, here are the first 30 digits of pi: 3.141592653 58979323846264338327 9.

HOW TO DO IT

1 Let's assume you can remember the beginning number 3 without any mental images. Then start to the right of the decimal place. Convert the following digits of pi into creative images.

2 Use the Chain Method (page 78) to connect the images together.

3 Keep going until you're sure you'll impress people. (Stop before people think you're weird.)

The following are examples using each method through 12 digits. Just continue the process if you want to do the entire 30 (or more).

RHYME TIME

Run-Door-Run-Hive-Sign-Chew-Tick-Hive-Tree-Hive-Bait-Sign . . .

Start with a pie. Imagine running (1) with it and smashing into a door (4). You get up and run (1) outside only to smash into a beehive (5). As you stand up you hit your head on the sign (9) reading "HONEY FOR SALE." Chew (2) on some honey that has ticks (6) in it. Put the honey back in the hive (5) and hang it from a branch in the tree (3), which suddenly falls over, smashing the hive (5). Worms/bait (8) form a sign (9) reading "Danger!"

THE MOST METHOD

14 to 15 = Yankees lose to the Red Sox in a heavy hitting game. 9:26 = I'm late for work but I made it before 9:30! 5:35 = I stayed 35 minutes

late to make up the time. $8.97 = I got a cheap dinner and I have three pennies rattling around in my pocket . . .

THE SIMPLE SYSTEM

1 (candle), 4 (chair), 1 (candle), 5 (fish), 9 (cat), 2 (shoes), 6 (ant), 5 (fish), 3 (tricycle), 5 (fish), 8 (octopus), 9 (cat) . . . Create your own story using these ideas.

THE MAJOR SYSTEM

Deer-doll-pine-seal-mail-fib (Pinocchio)-cape-moon-movie-rash-nosh . . .

The Major System uses two digits at a time, making it faster—after you invest the time to develop the system.

This is your chance to put your imagination to work. It might feel a little strange, but try it anyway. Once your mind starts to think this way, it gets easier to be more creative and to remember better.

TIP | YOUR NUMBER SYSTEM

Which number system is right for you? I present four systems in this book because so many people complain that numbers are hard to remember. If you prefer to make things up as you go, use the MOST Method. Otherwise, Rhyme Time is most people's favorite.

[39] Remember Your Lock Combination

AFTER MEMORIZING PI, your locker combination should be easy! But since the repercussions of not recalling the combination are worse than forgetting pi, it's important to do it right: Add details and review to remember. You'll then be able to open it when you're stressed, tired, or in a hurry.

Have you selected your favorite number system method yet? If not, please do so. Can't be bothered? Use the MOST Method (see page 22): Change the numbers into money, objects, sports scores, or time as you go—no work ahead of time required. You'll use your favorite number system to imagine the three sets of digits and combine them into a fun story that is easily remembered. By the way, make sure you have the combination. This technique can't help you recall numbers you once knew but have already forgotten, sorry!

HOW TO DO IT

1   Get the combination and write it down.

2   Translate the numbers into creative images. Don't forget to use CAST (**C**olor, **A**ction, **S**ize, and **T**exture).

3   Link the images together into a funny, memorable story. Keep adding more details until it's as clear in your mind as the last movie you saw.

4   Practice opening the lock three times *without* looking at the written combination. Use only your memory.

5   Practice opening the lock three more times from memory tomorrow morning.

6   When you have the combination committed to memory, store the written combination somewhere safe.

Here's an example:

Lock Combination: 16-01-12

THE MOST METHOD

16 = driving car; 01 = Mom is #1!; 12 = a dozen eggs

First day driving the car with Mom to the store to buy eggs. Add details like nearly getting into an accident, Mom trying to be supportive but terrified, and eggs flying out of the grocery bag and breaking all over the windshield.

Fun-Ticks; Hero-Fun; Fun-Chew

Playing ping-pong with a huge tick. My favorite superhero arrives and plays tetherball (another crazy-fun activity) with me. Later, we go back to ping-pong, but the superhero eats the ping-pong ball.

[40] Learn the Periodic Table of Elements

MEMORIZING THE PERIODIC table is a serious accomplishment. You could use rote memorization (boring and slow), a few funny songs (fun but not customizable), or the Accelerated Periodic Table (APT) Method. Guess which one I recommend? No matter which method you choose, it will require effort. The APT Method allows you to use your imagination so the material stays accessible far longer than the other methods.

THE TECHNIQUE ⁝ The APT Method

Memorizing the 118 elements in order by name, symbol, and number is relatively easy if you've paid attention to the techniques presented in the book so far. The APT Method is a combination of the CAR Method (see page 71) and the Chain Method (see page 78). The Link Method (see page 67), Memory Palace (see page 76), and Alphabet Images (see page 24) will also come into play to help you along.

The first major step is deciding how much you need to memorize. Remembering the elements by name in order while taking a moment to figure out the atomic number is the easiest and uses only one technique. Knowing the elements by group uses a similar technique with an additional element (sorry!). Finally, learning all the names, symbols, and numbers is possible using the same technique but with more detailed images.

1 Use the CAR Method and Chain Method to convert the 118 elements into images.

2 Use the Link Method to remember any symbols you may mix up (Au for gold, for example).

3 At every tenth element, add a mental marker by visualizing the image for the element flashing. You will be able to recall the atomic number by jumping through the links by 10 elements until you are near the one for which you need the number. For example:

> *Hydrogen = Kid waving "Hi!"*
>
> *Helium = Balloon. Connect the first two: the kid waves and lets go of the balloon.*
>
> *Lithium = Battery. Connect the balloon to a battery. The kid snatches the balloon and ties her phone (with a bulky battery) to the string.*
>
> *Beryllium = Bear. A bear takes the cell phone and the battery.*
>
> *Boron = Boring. The bear is bored by the phone and throws it into the street.*
>
> *Carbon = Car. A car runs over the phone.*
>
> *Nitrogen = Knight. A knight stops the car and climbs in.*
>
> *Oxygen = Oxygen. The knight stops at an oxygen bar.*
>
> *Fluorine = Floor. The knight reacts badly to the oxygen and falls to the floor.*
>
> *Neon = Neon sign. The sign on the wall (in neon) crashes to the floor. It flashes off and on, signaling that Neon's atomic number is 10.*

4   Repeat, making sure you link each previous element to the next one. All the symbols for the first 10 elements make sense and are easy to remember. When they don't, link the image with its symbol's Alphabet Image (see page 24). For potassium with the symbol K, link potassium (picture a banana or *pot*ato) with the Alphabet Image for K: kiwi.

5   To find the number for any element, count them from the start or find the nearest flashing element and count from there. For nitrogen, picture your image (knight), find it in your story chain, then find the nearest flashing element, which is three away at neon, so the number for nitrogen is 7 (10 minus 3).

APT METHOD 2

1   Use this same approach for remembering the elements by the eight main groups, with one addition: Start by imagining an anchor and connect that to the first element. (Note that this is easier in some ways: eight chains—one for each group—with each chain being much shorter than the 118-link chain for the first method.) Here's an example:

> *Anchor: Noble gases = King (a noble) with a green stinky gas around him.*
>
> *Helium: The first element. Connect the king with a balloon.*
>
> *Neon: Connect the balloon with a neon sign.*
>
> *Argon: Connect the sign with a pirate ("Arrrr").*
>
> *Krypton: Connect the pirate with a well-known superhero.*
>
> *Xenon: Connect the superhero with a well-known female warrior (Xena, Warrior Princess).*
>
> *Radon: Connect the warrior with a stingray.*

2 To remember the atomic number with this method, use one of the number systems you've learned to convert the number to an image. Add that image to the mix as you create your story: Helium (2) = the balloon has two shoes hanging from the string. Neon (10) has the most beautiful person in your world (a "perfect 10") holding up the neon sign. Argon (18) has the pirate driving an 18-wheeled tractor trailer.

3 Repeat for the other groups, making sure you start each group with the anchor image. To make sure you remember every group, connect the group images together in a group chain.

APT METHOD 3

Still with me? To learn the order, number, group, atomic mass, melting point, boiling point, when it's a liquid, or any other information, group them and make each character in your images very detailed. For example, in addition to the balloon (helium) with two shoes hanging off the string (atomic number 2), add a chair (4) with two donuts (00), a pair of shoes (2) and an ant (6) in that order on the seat to remember the atomic weight of 4.0026.

Yes, this method takes effort, but not nearly as much as rote memorization, and it's more flexible than using someone else's song. Commit 30 minutes to trying it. You'll be so far along—and it will be so memorable—you won't stop to do it any other way.

[41] Learn State and World Capitals

FOR A WELL-ROUNDED education, you want to have knowledge of state and world capitals. And if you're interested in travel, knowing this information can come in handy. However, you might want to learn the state and world capitals simply to exercise your memory. The CAR Method makes it quick and easy.

This is a simple yet powerful method to remember capital cities. All you need is your creativity! As you may remember from the earlier brain hack, the CAR Method follows this formula: 1) **C**onvert, 2) **A**ssociate, 3) **R**epeat. Imagine that you're driving your CAR around a map of the world and stopping at all the points of interest—in this case, the capitals.

HOW TO DO IT ⟩

1 Convert both the city and state or city and country into images based on the word itself or what it reminds you of.

2 Associate the two images using CAST (**C**olor, **A**ction, **S**ize, and **T**exture).

3 Repeat the images, adding details to make them even more memorable.

Here are a few examples.

Canberra, Australia

Convert. *What comes to mind when you think of Australia? Beaches, coral reef, kangaroos? Pick one and picture it. Next, convert Canberra into an image. This word makes me think of a cold can of soda (can-brr-a).*

Associate. *Kangaroo with a can (cold) of a drink.*

Repeat. *Add details. How does the kangaroo open and hold the can? What is the drink?*

Porto-Novo, Benin

Convert. *Benin ("beh-neen") reminds me of "baa" (sheep) and "knee." Porto-Novo makes me think of "pour-toe no-vote."*

Associate. The sheep with funny knees pours water on his toes, which disqualifies him from voting.

Repeat. Add details. Who was he going to vote for? What's up with those knees? Create a reason for the water on the toes.

Neither your images in step 1 nor your associations in step 2 have to be exact or even make much sense. They do have to be interesting enough to give your memory detective a few extra clues.

The same technique can be used for US state capitals.

Frankfort, Kentucky

Convert. Kentucky could be a "can" (that should be enough to remind you of the rest of the word). Frankfort is a "fort" made out of "franks" (hot dogs).

Associate. The can with the hot dog fort: Knock down the fort by tossing the can at it, open the can and have ants swarm out to eat the hot dogs, or whatever else your imagination creates.

Repeat. Add more details to make sure it sticks in your mind.

[42] Memorize Faster for Deadlines

THE FIRST TIME I tried to memorize a deck of cards in five minutes or less at a competition I failed. I couldn't do it that quickly. Now I can remember a deck of cards in less than 60 seconds. I'll show you my hack here.

Do you need to remember information in a hurry? You can do it. It's best if you have a solid foundation in these techniques, so I hope you're not reading this hack the night before your final exam! Even without much practice, though, it can work.

Your mind is faster and better at remembering than you realize, so pushing yourself to go faster will lead to surprising results. You should already have experience converting what you're learning into exaggerated, interesting images. The more you practice the CAR Method (see page 71) or the Chain Method (see page 78), the faster you'll get at providing clues for your memory detective.

Have your notes, mind map, or material already prepared. You'll also need a countdown timer and a willingness to push yourself! The method is to either "speed convert" essential information into images or, if you are reviewing, speed through the mental images you previously created and add more crazy details. After, you'll test yourself to force your mind to recall.

HOW TO DO IT >

1   Plan your study session. How long do you have? How many 10-minute sessions can you do? Plan around that. For the first session, set a countdown timer for 5 minutes.

2   Choose a page, section, list, or chapter that seems too much to learn (or review) in 5 minutes.

3   Start the timer and buzz through the material. Push yourself. Go faster than you think you'll be able to remember. Make it a game: How fast can you go?

4   To learn for the first time: Translate everything you want to remember into an image and connect it to something. Picture the question and the answer and connect them together, put the information into a Memory Palace (see page 76), or connect the ideas to one another using the Chain Method.

5   To review the information again: See the images you've already created, reviewing the connections and unique stories.

6   Don't slow down even if you feel you aren't getting the information. Trust the speed of your mind.

7   When the timer ends, stop and restart the timer for another 5 minutes. Close your eyes (or cover part of the page), and immediately test your memory. Testing yourself so soon after looking at the material instead of waiting until the end of your study session is better for remembering.

Whether you remember everything or not, don't worry. When the timer goes off, mark any problem areas with a highlighter or red pen (using a different color than usual is important). Don't review or learn while marking. Just note the parts you struggled with and move on.

8   Continue with another section: Spend 5 minutes learning or reviewing more information than you think you can remember, then do 5 minutes of testing, followed by quickly marking the areas you didn't remember when you tested yourself.

9   Toward the end of your study session, set your timer for 5 minutes and review all the areas highlighted or marked from the beginning of the study session to the end. Go as fast as you can. Reset the timer and test yourself for 5 minutes, then mark anything you still aren't getting with a *different* colored pen or highlighter.

10   Slow down and focus on the parts you didn't learn. Review this book for a technique that may help. If you've used a technique and it isn't working, are your images exaggerated and have enough wild details? Boring is forgettable; wild is memorable. Make sure your creative pictures and stories are as strange or silly as possible.

11   Take a short break. Close your eyes and relax. Don't read, watch TV, worry, or think about the material. Rest. Let your mind process behind the scenes.

12   Repeat as needed depending on the amount of material and time available.

[43] Prepare for Important Exams

WHEN IT'S TIME to hit the books to prepare for the GRE, ACT, SAT, or another important exam, it's time to get serious about remembering large amounts of data as quickly, easily, and efficiently as possible. There are only a certain number of hours available to study, so you need to use them wisely. The 42 brain hacks you've learned so far will allow you to maximize your time. You'll learn and review in ways that make information "sticky" so you can easily recall it during your big test.

THE TECHNIQUE : Combine Methods to Excel

Entrance exams don't test pure memorization, but it helps to know as much as possible. Many exams require an excellent vocabulary. Some require knowledge of math concepts and formulas (see page 96 for this). All require effective study methods to pass. Thankfully, you've already learned four tools to master a large amount of test preparation material:

1 The CAR Method (page 71)
2 The Chain Method (page 78)
3 The Link Method (page 67)
4 Memory Palace (page 76)

Combining these methods and using the study techniques presented earlier makes studying for a big exam manageable.

HOW TO DO IT

1 With your test prep book in hand, use the concepts in the hack Memorize Faster for Deadlines on page 91 to quickly scan entire sections, learning and testing yourself as you go. This will give you an indication of where you need to spend the most time.

2 Improve your vocabulary. Skip to Vocabulary Improvement for Business Success (page 120) and read that hack. Apply the CAR Method to learning as many words per day as you can. Set a goal, work the method, and achieve it daily.

3 For learning or reviewing massive amounts of detailed information, create multiple Memory Palaces. Use your current home, first home, favorite shopping mall, a store, a park, a sports stadium, school classrooms, or the library. Pick any place you can easily picture and see in your mind.

For example, if you're preparing for the MCAT, designate certain rooms in your childhood home as the areas for storing the physical topics of living systems. Every piece of information could be imagined, creatively connected to its associated concepts, and pictured in detail. If you're stumped for an answer about this subject at test time, you would know to "look" in your living room, for example, and "see" the general topic and specific details.

a] Select 10 locations per room or main area by standing in the doorway (if it's a room) and looking left (clockwise is generally easier than counterclockwise, but use whatever works for the particular place). The first location will be the wall or corner nearest the door. What's there? A lamp, table, plant? That's #1. The next location is the following wall or corner. Whatever major item in that space is #2. Continue until you have 10 spots, using wall-corner-wall-corner. Finish with the ceiling (#9) and the middle of the floor (#10).

b] Write down the name of the Memory Palace and itemize the locations. Review forward and backward several times until you know the locations easily. It sounds like a lot of prep work, but it's easy once you've done it a few times. And when you start to store information in the locations, it becomes apparent how powerful this technique is. Suddenly you can organize, save, and recall massive amounts of data.

[44] Remember Formulas for Exams

REMEMBERING FORMULAS SOUNDS incredibly hard and boring, but it doesn't have to be. Your imagination is the key to making anything easy and fun to remember. Let's look at some common formulas for the GRE and other exams here. Save yourself time and study better by taking the time to commit them to memory.

Remember, the mind loves images and finds them easy to recall. Anything can be converted into an image by asking what it reminds you of. Then it's merely a matter of connecting the images together into a story or movie that is unique enough to be memorable.

THE TECHNIQUE • Items Interact

This method is simply converting everything in a formula to a picture, then using your imagination to see them interacting. An easy formula you may already know is the area of a circle: $A = \pi r^2$.

How do you remember that? *A* for area is easy. Pi can be easily pictured with your favorite type of pie. *R* stands for radius but could be *rat* or *robot*. Multiplication is implied and can either be remembered in context or converted to an image: "times" can be a clock or, as I think of it, hitting the other item. The image for the formula for area becomes pie hitting two rats—one is on the other one's shoulders to represent *squared*. You could also place them inside a box to represent *square* or even leave that part out, because your natural memory will fill it in for you.

HOW TO DO IT

1 **Make sure you understand the formula. There is a big difference between memorizing something and knowing how it works. Use this hack to help you learn faster and understand more.**

2 **Write out the formula in words that make sense.**

3 **Convert the words into images. Creatively make the images interact.**

4 **Review and add details.**

Here are a few examples.

CIRCUMFERENCE: $C = \text{o}(2r)$ or $\text{o}d$

> *The distance around something (like a circle) equals pi times (two times the radius), or pi times the diameter.*

> *Imagine the circumference (I see a circle) being the same as a pie hitting two rats or a pie hitting one diamond.*

DISTANCE, RATE, AND TIME

> $d = rt$

> *Distance is how far away I am from a rat.*

> *You might be given the distance and time and be asked for the rate. Here's the formula:*

> $r = d/t$

> *rate = distance divided by time*

> *How fast is the rat compared to the dog trying to get over the fence (/) to the turkey?*

THE AREA OF A TRIANGLE

> $\frac{1}{2} bh$

> *One-half base times height*

> *How much can you fit into a triangle? Imagine a triangle and cramming in one half of a banana by hitting it with the hamburger that also gets shoved in.*

Using this method almost seems like cheating, but it's just being smart. Make the math part of the exams easy by memorizing the formulas while you learn to use them. It will give you confidence to face the exams head-on.

[45] Remember Your Class Schedule

A NEW SEMESTER, a new class schedule. It's not a big problem if you have only a few classes, but what if you have several classes, labs, a work schedule, and other recurring items to remember? Memory hacks to the rescue! For the best results, I recommend creating your own system, but if mine makes sense, use it or modify it as needed.

THE TECHNIQUE ⦙ The Days of the Week System

The basic technique has several parts. There is a small learning curve, and it may seem complicated at first. But if you have a full schedule to commit to memory quickly, this will save you time, effort, and the embarrassment of losing track of where you're supposed to be.

Each day is assigned an image that makes it easy to remember. I recommend using people or characters that remind you of the day of the week. For time, you can use one of the number systems: Rhyme Time (see page 33), the Simple System (see page 25), the Major System (see page 35), or the MOST Method (see page 22). Or you can use blocks: morning, midmorning, lunch, early afternoon, late afternoon, and evening. Each of those gets an image to go with it. Then you translate your schedule into images, connecting them to form a memorable story for each event.

HOW TO DO IT ⟩

1   List the days of the week and create a system so that you can easily imagine each weekday as a character. Here's an example:

Monday	Moon-day	Astronaut
Tuesday	Two's day	Toddler (terrible twos) crying and throwing a tantrum
Wednesday	Wedding day	Bride in a beautiful white dress
Thursday	Thor's day	Thor with his hammer
Friday	Fry day	Fried food = a fry cook with dirty apron
Saturday	Saturn day	Alien
Sunday	Sun day	Animated sun character

2 To remember the time of each event, you can decide on a number system. For example, if your first class is at 9 a.m., you might be able to remember the time by picturing a pile of pancakes for "breakfast" as a reminder while your natural memory fills in the 9 a.m. detail. If that doesn't work or you need the exact number, picture a cat (for its "nine lives") and associate it with the day of the week.

3 Go through your calendar and create your schedule by translating everything into creative images and combine, adding exaggerated details as you go.

Here's an example:

Monday		
10:00	Biochem	Astronaut with "perfect 10" model pouring liquid from a test tube into beaker together
1:30	Anatomy	Astronaut examining body parts while on a TV behind him your team loses 1 to 30
4:00	Work at restaurant	Astronaut golfing (4 = "fore!") at the restaurant where you work
8:00	Study group	Astronaut studying with an octopus

Tuesday		
11:15	Lab	Grumpy toddler pays $11.15 to get into a lab to play with test tubes
3:00	Calculus	Toddler rides a tricycle (3) over a calculator
5:30	Work at restaurant	Toddler runs a 5:30 mile around the inside of your restaurant

The challenge with this system is creating it the first time. After you use it once, it becomes second nature and can keep you from losing track of where you're supposed to be.

[46] Ace Anatomy and Physiology

YOU'RE TAKING ANATOMY and Physiology? Don't panic! Memory techniques work very well with this material. I first detailed the CAR Method on page 71 for remembering foreign languages. Here I have modified it for definitions, body functions, and more—which, when you think about it, are like learning words in a foreign language. Use it to drive your way to success in this challenging class.

THE TECHNIQUE : Convert and Associate

As you've learned, CAR stands for **C**onvert, **A**ssociate, and **R**eview. You will be converting each word, suffix, prefix, or body part into an image. Then you'll convert each definition, meaning, or other detail into its own image. Next, you'll associate them by making up a memorable image or mini movie. Exaggeration pays off here—the mind remembers the strange, silly, unique, upside-down, oversized, and colorful details very well. Review the wild image or movie, adding more details by using CAST (**C**olor, **A**ction, **S**ize, and **T**exture).

Keep in mind that most information can be saved in your memory by reading the textbook, participating in the lectures, and doing the homework. This method is best used for information you don't naturally remember using the study strategies, FIT Method (see page 61), and your natural memory ability.

HOW TO DO IT

1 Convert each part into an image. For example, you need to remember "medial," and the definition is "toward the midline of the body." Break it down to *me* and *dial* (you dialing a phone) and picture a line on the center of your body to remember "toward the midline of the body."

2 Associate the two images together in a strange, silly way. The line through the center of your body has the phone keypad near it and you ("me") dial your phone using the keypad on your stomach.

3 Repeat, adding details. What color is the line running down your body? Is it thick? Thin? Imagine having to poke the middle of your body every time you need to dial your phone. Are you ticklish? Close your eyes and imagine everything in great detail.

Here's an example:

METABOLISM = ANABOLISM AND CATABOLISM PROCESSES

Anabolism is the process of smaller molecules combining into larger, more complex substances. *Catabolism* is the process of more complex substances that are broken into simpler, smaller molecules.

1 Convert all the words into images:

- Metabolism = Mets baseball team playing with a ball.
- Anabolism = "An a" (an apple) or "Anna," which always reminds me of "banana" = a banana playing with a ball that rolls around collecting bits and pieces of the ground, growing bigger and more complex.
- Catabolism = a cat playing with a ball that gets pieces torn off as it gets broken into simpler, smaller parts.

2 Associate the words together, this time using the Chain Method (see page 78): Create a movie of the cat and banana both playing with the balls. See the Mets being so interested in the game that they draft the cat and banana to bring the game to New York.

3 Add details. The cat is orange and large like a tiger, and the banana is blue and as big as a baseball bat. They fit right in with the Mets.

[47] Remember Any Recipe

DO YOU LOVE to cook or bake but find yourself tied to your cookbooks? Memorizing recipes makes life easier even if you're not a professional chef. First, define what you want: Do you find yourself knowing most of the recipe but forgetting certain parts or measurements? Do you need to remember the ingredients so you know what to buy at the store? Do you want to memorize the entire recipe from ingredients to measurements? Your answer may differ for different types of recipes—baking a cake versus making dinner, for example. No matter what, though, you can easily remember recipes with this memory hack.

The Recipe System is used for remembering the measurements and steps of any recipe. You can adopt my system or modify it to make it your own. This system requires that each measurement have an associated image, like this:

- Cup—Fist or hand (approximate measurement of a cup)
- ⅛ cup—Octopus with teacups
- ¼ cup—A quarter coin or a horse ("quarter horse")
- ½ cup—A mug cut vertically in half
- ⅓ cup—Mp3 player (phone), headphones, or 3-D movie glasses
- ¾ cup—Tricycle (three wheels), three little pigs
- Teaspoon—Index finger (approximate measurement of a teaspoon)
- ⅛ teaspoon—Octopus with spoons
- ¼ teaspoon—House (four walls)
- ½ teaspoon—Peace sign (2 fingers)
- ¾ teaspoon—Pyramid or triangle (three sides)
- Tablespoon—Thumb (approximate measurement of a tablespoon)
- ½ tablespoon—Spoon with a hole in it

Try these or create your own that make sense. If you commonly use one that isn't listed, create an image or pick a random cooking image (like a spatula) and assign it. Processes need to be imagined also but should be easy, as simmer, boil, roast, bake, or broil can be pictured—or is usually obvious in context.

HOW TO DO IT ⟩

1 Select a recipe you'd like to memorize.

2 Read through it twice, and then close your eyes and test yourself. What parts are hard to remember?

3   Convert what you couldn't remember into mental images using my system or your own.

4   Use one of the number systems to remember amounts such as "2 cups" = fists (cup) combined with shoes (2).

5   Link everything together using the Chain Method (see page 78) to remember the order of the steps.

6   Review the recipe while adding details to your mental story or movie.

7   Make the dish from memory, looking at the recipe only if absolutely necessary. Forcing your mind to recall it will help you remember it better next time.

8   Enjoy your food!

This is much easier to do in practice than it is to read. There are only a few images to master, and if mine don't speak to you, just think of ones that do. Give this a try with a recipe that often trips you up and enjoy the feeling of finally knowing it by heart.

TIP | WHAT ABOUT THE INGREDIENTS?

Use the Chain Method to first think of an image of the dish, and then create exaggerated images of each ingredient, connecting everything like links in a chain. Don't simply picture a stick of butter or a bag of sugar. Imagine a six-foot-tall stick of butter that makes the floor of the grocery store aisle slippery, and see yourself sprinkling sugar from a 40-pound bag onto the floor so people don't fall. You might need to dust it with flower petals (instead of just picturing flour) to make it more fun to walk on. Everything must be strange and wild to be memorable or the technique will not work!

[48] Remember Your Lines for a Play

THE ROAR OF the crowd after a well-done performance is wonderful. But the fear of forgetting your next line has kept many would-be stars from experiencing the joys of performing. A live performance is a true test of memory ability under pressure. Given enough time and effort, it's possible to use rote memorization to learn your character's lines, but learning them quickly gives you more time to work on your acting. These memory hacks make it possible.

THE TECHNIQUE • Identify Problem Areas

Thankfully the lines in plays (usually) make sense. Story, emotion, and characters come together to play off one another. By reading your part, you naturally start to imagine the scenes, which helps you remember what to say. Step one to remembering your lines is to read them, do the work of imagining the scene, understand why your character is saying the lines, and get a sense of which parts are easy for you to remember.

The next step is applying memory hacks to parts that concern you. These are often when your character starts the scene with limited context to remind you of what happens next, tricky dialogue, or soliloquies. Use this hack to speed up the process of knowing your lines by heart and to reassure yourself. In an emergency, you have a reminder prepared in your mind for lines you are concerned you might forget.

HOW TO DO IT

1 Read the script and analyze your parts. Identify the lines or sections that seem hard to remember.

2 Often all our minds need is a nudge in the right direction to get started. For the first line in a scene, a part that trips you up, or to remember multiple long lines, convert the first few words into images and add them to the scene in your mind. Here's an example:

In *Romeo and Juliet,* the Prince enters and begins a 23-line speech. Change the first few words into images and link them together to give your mind a cue for each part.

    a] *Rebellious subjects, enemies to peace:* Your favorite rebel; pick one from the group of characters onstage.

    b] *Profaners of this neighbour-stained steel:* "Profaner" is one letter away from "profanger," like Dracula with his steel that is stained by the blood of his neighbors he's drained. Imagine one of the other actors as Dracula.

    c] *Will they not hear? What, ho! you men, you beasts:* William Tell = apple, or imagine another actor onstage with his last will and testament pinned to a bale of hay (they) balanced by his ear (hear).

    d] *That quench the fire of your pernicious rage:* That = fat from meat sizzling on ("quenching") a fire.

3 Remember out of context. Have a friend or scene partner choose a line prior to one of yours—from anywhere in the play—and read it out loud. Force your mind to find your line out of context.

4 Go backward. Don't say the sentences backward, only the order of the lines. Start at the end of the play and recall each section backward. Doing the play in reverse with a scene partner creates more pathways to form the memory of the lines.

5 Practice transitions. Professional musicians may practice the first few notes of a particularly tough section to get the nuances just right. Practice any transitions or other areas that you frequently have trouble remembering.

6 Write out the first letter of each line or section that you struggle with. Use it as a key to test whether you remember each word perfectly. Write out and read "R-s-e-t-p / p-o-t-n-s-s" as an aid to learning the line.

With these hacks, you'll be on your way to fame and fortune in no time. When you get there, remember the little people who helped you (like me!).

[49] Remember Religious or Spiritual Passages

DO YOU PRACTICE your faith by memorizing spiritual passages? For some people, rote memorization is fine. For them, reading the words over and over not only helps them memorize but also provides a sense of spiritual connection. Others use memory techniques to remember more quickly than the rote memorization method allows for. They prefer to know the passage and dwell on them as they commute, walk in nature, or at other times when their holy book is unavailable.

THE TECHNIQUE : Use the First Few Words

The method for remembering religious or spiritual passages is easy. First, decide if you need help remembering the exact passage word for word or if you need a simple cue, like the first few words, to remember verbatim. You may also need to remember a few words that you tend to misremember. Next, decide if you also would like to know the chapter and verse or other passage number. If so, I suggest learning the Major System (see page 35) to be able to quickly connect the numbers to the image of the first few words of the passage or line.

HOW TO DO IT

1 Read the passage and convert it into a story using your creativity. Translate a few keywords to provide a cue for recall. Here's an example:

> **NIV Bible**
>
> *Consider it pure joy, my brothers and sisters, whenever you face trials of many kinds.*
> *(James 1:2)*

I imagine my brothers and sisters in a circle, considering a broken computer (trial and IT) with pure joy on their faces, with one looking at her watch ("whenever" and "face"), when a kind judge walks in (trials of many kinds). Often the first word may be enough to remind you of the passage. If I had trouble getting started, since the overall picture is not a word-for-word, I would add that the judge could be thought of as a convict ("con") babysitter ("sider").

2   To remind yourself of a passage you already know verbatim, translate the essence of the passage into an image as you did in step 1. If you've already committed the passage to memory through study, you probably have the image in your mind. Strengthen it by adding details or putting yourself into the scene.

3   To learn a passage word for word, first read it three times, close your eyes, and test yourself. What words do you naturally remember and what do you forget? If you forget only a few words, which is common, change each frequently forgotten word into a picture and connect it to the image of the story that relates to the passage.

4   To cue your memory for some passage, you may need to change many smaller words into images. Create them as you go or imagine them ahead of time, assigning images to each. Here are a few suggestions—use them or modify them as needed. Some of these might not make much sense to you, because this is my system where I've decided on images because they rhyme, what the word looks like to me, or my own a random assignment.

Word	Image Ideas
The	tea (cup or bag)
An	nun
And	Andy or nod (head)
That	bat
In	sign for a hotel (inn)
He	generic man or man specific to the passage
For	related to golfing ("Fore!") created in the moment by context
Shall	shell
To	movement or direction or shoes ("to" rhymes with "shoe")

5   To learn the numbers associated with each passage, take the time to completely prepare your Major System. This makes it easy to connect the number images with the images for each line or verse.

6   See "Remember Your Lines for a Play" on page 104 for more ideas such as working with a partner to remember better.

Working on this method is a wonderful way to strengthen your faith and your memory at the same time.

[50] How to Be a Memory Athlete

"WHY IN THE world would anyone want to be a memory athlete?!" Does the idea of sitting in a room memorizing things with other people sound boring? Don't worry, I completely understand, but hear me out! Becoming a memory athlete is like running a 5K race or joining a softball league. It's a way to improve fitness (mental in this case) while being surrounded by other fun people with a similar interest. It has many advantages.

- Everyday memory greatly improves
- The ability to focus and tune out distractions increases
- It is surprisingly enjoyable
- Non-memory athletes think you're a genius just for participating
- There is camaraderie with others interested in memory improvement

Read this section with an open mind. I'd love to see you at the next competition.

THE TECHNIQUE : A Small Amount of Practice

As an amateur memory athlete, you will use the same systems, methods, and techniques you've been learning throughout this book. The only difference between a person who wants to remember better and a memory athlete is the amount of practice.

At memory competitions, there are anywhere from four to ten different events. Here's the amazing part: You already have 99 percent of the information you need just from reading this book to enter and do well at a memory competition.

In this book I don't go into detail to describe the systems for memorizing a deck of cards or binary numbers, but with a bit of practice and a few Memory Palaces (see page 76), you're already ready. Don't forget it's not about rote memorization; all the methods needed for competitive memorizing rely on creating odd, funny images or mental movies to remember the information. The most common events at competitions are:

- **NAMES AND FACES.** Pictures of people and names from all over all the world.
- **RANDOM NUMBERS.** This can be memorizing an 80-digit number in under one minute, five minutes to memorize as much of a 600-digit number as possible, or longer events of up to 60 minutes of memorizing hundreds of digits.
- **PLAYING CARDS.** Memorize a shuffled deck of playing cards as fast as possible (or as much of a deck as you can) in under five minutes, or enjoy the longer events where you memorize as many decks of cards as you can in one hour.
- **BINARY NUMBERS.** Memorize 10011011000110101011001... for 30 fun-filled minutes.
- **RANDOM WORDS.** Memorize columns of words for 15 minutes.
- **SPOKEN NUMBERS.** A computerized voice speaks one random digit per second. The numbers are never seen (and of course competitors are not allowed to write them down). This is my favorite event and the one where I set the United States record two years in a row (112 digits, then 150 digits).
- **RANDOM IMAGES.** Photos of random scenes like a sunset, bird, bridge, road, flowers, balloon, etc. are displayed and their order must be memorized.

1   Check out these two websites dedicated to helping people train as memory athletes: Memoryleague.com and Memocamp.com.

2   Start with the Names and Faces event first. It's practical in real life and doesn't require Memory Palaces or specific systems.

3   Develop at least three Memory Palaces (page 76) with 10 locations each. Then try the random images event or random words using your Memory Palaces to store the information.

4   Do a little practice several times a week, enjoying both the challenge and the feeling of accomplishment.

5   Pick a competition and go for it. The website Memoryleague .com has a head-to-head competition feature—you don't even have to leave your home to compete, and matches take as little as four minutes.

6   To learn more about the sport and see a list of competitions, visit http://www.iam-memory.org.

3

Work

By now you've seen how powerful these hacks can be. Keep reading to discover how you can amaze your coworkers, bosses, managers, or clients. Even if you're not working at a traditional nine-to-five job, I encourage you to read this part anyway to discover more techniques that can be applied to other areas of life besides the workplace.

[51] Surprising Memory Habits for Business & Sales Success

WE ALL HAVE habits. The question is, Are they helping us get where we want to go or holding us back? If you've ever worked with someone who is "sharp" and "with it," you know how impressive they can seem, especially if we feel we don't compare favorably. Do yourself the favor of developing good memory habits that impress people.

These specific memory habits can be used daily to strengthen your mind and assist in your pursuit of a better memory.

THE TECHNIQUE ┊ Back Up Your Important Memories

I'm a fan of writing down important details, which may seem strange to read in a book about memory hacks. My philosophy is that business is too important to be left only to memory. Our memory should be the main way to keep track of things, but when money is on the line—our own or that of our clients'—using a secondary method is important. We back up the essential information on our computers, so let's back up our minds, too.

The first memory habit, then, is the Brain Dump. The next is using Checklists, and the last is to Reduce Stress. Develop the habit of using these techniques. They all help your memory by reviewing important details, cleaning up clutter in the mind, organizing thoughts, and relieving worries.

HOW TO DO IT

1 **THE BRAIN DUMP. Getting all the important details out of our heads and into a customer relationship manager, a database, meeting notes, or a simple daily journal helps tremendously. Writing or typing out the information tells our minds to pay attention, as this material is obviously important. We learned the material once with the client or during the course of business, and now we're documenting it. The mind thinks, "I've got to pay attention to this!"**

   Your method will vary depending on your business, but make detailed notes toward the end of every day. If you're

too busy or writing isn't your favorite, talk to a coworker or partner about the important points or simply review your day mentally as you commute.

2 **CHECKLISTS.** Pilots use checklists even after they've flown thousands of times. If your work involves something important—and what work doesn't?—create and use checklists. Having them will help your mind focus and, interestingly, free up space in your mind to remember things you might have otherwise missed. A checklist can also help reduce stress. Your mind can find peace because it no longer has to go over and over details, wondering if it's forgetting anything important.

3 **STRESS RELIEF.** We all know self-care is good for us, but how many of us follow through and make it a habit? Pick something—whether it's yoga or jujitsu—and put it onto your calendar. "I'll get around to it" hasn't been working, has it? It only creates more stress. If you need more motivation, use the SPEAR Technique on page 56.

The punitive approach is especially effective with businesspeople and salespeople: Get a sizable amount of cash and write a note saying, "Thanks for your wonderful work!" Address it to an organization you loathe. Give it to a trusted friend. If you don't go to four yoga classes this month or run a certain number of miles, your friend will mail it for you. This can also be used per week or per activity with smaller dollar amounts. While this is a good motivator, make sure it doesn't backfire and create more stress than it relieves!

[52] Remember Computer Shortcuts

BEING ABLE TO rely on your memory saves time and improves efficiency. Remembering keyboard shortcuts may seem minor, but considering all the time you spend at your computer, the seconds you save add up, especially when using software with many available time-saving shortcuts. Many video, photo, and audio editing software make extensive use of keyboard shortcuts, as do database and writing programs.

This memory hack can be put into practice nearly instantly. Use it as a short-term technique to bridge the gap between learning the shortcut and making it part of your keyboard repertoire or to remember infrequently used shortcuts to have ready for the rare times you need them.

THE TECHNIQUE ⋮ Time-Saving System

Keyboard shortcuts rely almost exclusively on holding down a few main keys, like the control and shift keys, then pressing another key like a letter or symbol. All that's needed for your shortcut system is to create mental images of the main keys. The second key pressed will usually make sense: <Control> F for find will be easy to remember. If not, you will use an Alphabet Image (see page 24) to make it stick.

HOW TO DO IT ⟩

1 Choose your image for each main shortcut key. These are mine:

PC	
Control	Airplane (contrail)—picture a pilot
Shift	Makes letters bigger (capitalization), so picture a giant
Function	Sounds like "fun" (picture something fun) or "luncheon" (a chef, plates, etc.)
Windows symbol	Bill Gates, or a window
Alt	Owl, ant, or car battery ("alternator")

Mac	
Shift	Makes letters bigger (capitalization), so picture a giant
Command	In command (picture a military commander like a general)
Control	Reminds me of an airplane (contrail), so picture a pilot, or "king" (the symbol on the key reminds me of a crown)
Option	Reminds me of "operation" (picture a doctor) or a child (the symbol on the key reminds me of a playground slide)

2 Imagine the keyboard shortcut by what it does or a reminder based on the letter pressed.

3 Combine the main key's image with an image of the second key (and third in some cases) by using Alphabet Images (page 24). Sometimes it's easier to start with the main key image, add the second key image, then create a little story to associate the idea of the shortcut.

Here are a few examples:

To hide everything on your computer screen, minimizing all windows:

PC: Alt + F	Owl flies away with your computer screen
Mac: Command + H	A general hops on your computer screen, making everything vanish

To access the emojis available from the keyboard:

PC: WIN + Period	Bill Gates hits a nail (period) along with his finger and makes a painful emoji face
Mac: Control + Command + Space Bar	Pilot and general are in space: see their emoji expressions

To paste from a website or other document without keeping the original formatting:

PC: Control + Shift + V	Pilot and giant drive a van with plain text on the sides
Mac: Shift + Command + V	Giant and general drive a van with boring writing on the sides

The process is simple and requires only a few basic mental images to make it work. It makes the process of remembering large amounts of shortcuts much faster.

TIP | "HOW WILL I REMEMBER THAT?"

When confronted with something you want to remember, ask yourself, "How will I remember that?" Stopping to ask the question brings your attention to the moment. It also helps you think of exactly which system, method, or technique to use, and improves memory instantly.

[53] Memorize Large Amounts of New Information Quickly

STARTING A NEW job can be exciting, stressful, and—of course—a memory challenge. There are new names to remember, procedures to follow, and often large amounts of new information to learn. Memory techniques help shorten the time between not having a clue and knowing everything cold. Keep in mind the premise of this book: Remembering well is possible. It's not a mystical process that only super-humans can do. It's not even especially difficult. Work with your mind and use the techniques described. You'll be impressing your new coworkers (and managers) in no time.

THE TECHNIQUE ⁝ Select the Best Technique

You have the strategies and skills needed to impress everyone at your new job with how quickly you learn. Here are suggestions for strategies to use based on some common things you may need to learn:

- Remember Names (page 11)
- Remember Details of Clients, Prospects, and Coworkers (page 134)
- Remember Entire Books (page 62)
- Remember a Series of Items Like the Bill of Rights (page 78)
- Remember Speeches and Presentations (page 121)

Also review A Better Memory Every Morning on page 6 and the Toothbrushing Review on page 21 to prepare for your first days and weeks at your new job.

HOW TO DO IT

APPROACH 1

1   Help your mind so your natural memory ability is free to shine. Use memory techniques for remembering more than your mind would normally be able to manage.

2   Start by working *with* your mind instead of *against* it.
    This includes the "low-hanging fruit" of getting enough
    sleep, eating well, and exercising. Even more important
    are managing stress and focusing. Review the sections in
    the book that discuss these issues, especially Prepare Your
    Mind for Tests on page 64, which is about relaxing in the
    face of a difficult situation. Starting a new job is stressful,
    and every day can feel like test day!

APPROACH 2

There always seems to be one person whose name is hard to remember, a specific procedure that doesn't make sense or doesn't stick in the mind, or details that you have trouble getting exactly right. When that happens, remember to drive your way to success with CAR (see page 71):

1   **C**onvert anything you have trouble remembering into a silly,
    exaggerated image. Make it huge, colorful, and active.

2   **A**ssociate it with either another image (connect the
    question and answer or the name and face) or a Memory
    Palace (see page 76). You can use your vehicle Memory
    Palace for short-term help or create work-specific ones
    for longer-term storage (your new office or building, for
    example, would be a great place to store work-related
    creative images).

3   **R**eview the images and resulting associations, adding
    details. Additionally, mentally review the images for
    important information two or three times per day at first
    until they are solidly stored in your long-term memory.
    I suggest reviewing at mealtimes as well as when you brush
    your teeth each morning and evening.

[54] Vocabulary Improvement for Business Success

YOUR VOCABULARY SAYS a lot about you. Having the right word, at the right time, and using it correctly impresses others and makes communication easier. Using the wrong word or pronouncing it incorrectly, though, can be embarrassing. I once used the word *epitome* but mispronounced it "ep-i-tome." I still remember the look on the other person's face—they thought I was an idiot! This memory hack is an outstanding way to confidently expand your vocabulary to stand out in any business environment (in a good way!).

THE TECHNIQUE ⋮ The CAR Method Plus Vocabulary Words

Learning vocabulary words is the same as learning foreign words, only easier. You'll use the CAR Method again: **C**onverting the word and the definition into images, **A**ssociating them in a creative way, and then **R**epeating the association with additional details to make it more memorable.

My recommendation is a page-a-day calendar with a new vocabulary word to learn each day. If you can't get one of those, look online for lists of words every adult should know. Pick one (or more) each day and use the CAR Method (see page 71) to start impressing people in just a few days.

HOW TO DO IT

1 Convert the word (focusing on pronunciation, if necessary) and the word's meaning into images.

2 Associate the images with each other.

3 Repeat, adding details.

Here are two examples:

Innate: inborn, something one has since birth

Pronunciation: in-ate

She has an innate talent for drawing.

1　Convert: *In-ate* = in + eight = inside of an octopus (eight arms). Convert the definition: often a talent like drawing or musical ability or even getting oneself into trouble.

2　A talented young artist drawing a SCUBA diver with his arm caught inside an octopus.

3　Repeat, adding details.

> *Egregious: shockingly bad*
>
> *Pronunciation: ah-gre-geus*
>
> *He made an egregious error when he served steak to the vegetarian.*

Looking at the pronunciation and definition should spark your creativity. When it does, the images come together quickly without necessarily having to complete every step.

1–2　Convert and associate as you go: *ah-gre-geus* into "ahh" (mouth inspected at the doctor), "gre" (green), "geus" (just), which equals the patient saying "Ahh" for the doctor who sees that "just" part of the mouth is green. The doctor notes this an egregious issue.

3　Repeat with more details. "But Doc, it's 'geus' part of my mouth!"

This process is enjoyable and benefits your career. To make it even easier, pair up with a friend or group. It can be hilarious to hear how other people convert words and meanings into images.

[55] Remember Speeches & Presentations

ONE OF THE most frightening and stressful activities is public speaking. So much can and often does go wrong. I've seen people drop their carefully written and ordered notecards, forget their glasses and be unable to read their notes, and practice so much they don't think they need any notes at all only to completely forget everything.

With your natural memory, assisted by a few simple techniques, you won't need notes and won't blank out. Imagine being able to speak with confidence—from memory. People will be impressed and think you're a genius.

THE TECHNIQUE A Memory Palace for Your Speech

By now you have a lot of experience converting words and ideas into creative mental pictures. To remember speeches, you'll convert your main points into images. You could associate them with each other with the Chain Method (page 78), but there's a better method for speeches. It uses the Memory Palace (see page 76) to store your main points.

If you forget one link with the Chain Method, the rest of the speech could be lost. Using the Memory Palace allows for the possibility of missing one point but still being able to complete the rest of the speech. Since public speaking is so stressful for many people, it's better to learn and practice this method. It's safer in the long run.

HOW TO DO IT

1   To begin you will create a Memory Palace with enough rooms to store every main point of your speech. This doesn't have to be difficult. A Memory Palace is only a series of locations you can easily imagine—*in order.* Use a piece of paper to create this, as you may need to refer to it a few times later as you practice.

2   Imagine your home. Where do you enter it? That's location one. Write "1" and the place, like "front door." What is the next major room or area? That's location two. Write it down.

3   Continue through your home. I prefer moving clockwise, so if you're confronted with a choice of the bathroom on the left and the kitchen on the right, put the bathroom as the next room, and then the kitchen. However, it's your mind and your Memory Palace. Write down the areas in the order that makes sense to you. Use major spaces like rooms, aiming for 10 to 20 locations. Some large rooms could have

two areas, like the kitchen cooking area and the breakfast nook or table on the opposite wall.

4 Finish writing down your Memory Palace, and then close your eyes and mentally walk through it. Do you naturally envision the same path? If not, fix it so you do, and then mentally review it once more. Is the path easy to remember and each space obvious? Keep reviewing, fixing as needed, until your mental walk-through visualizes the same spaces in the same order every time.

5 Convert the main points of your speech into mental images or cues, the same way you'd summarize the point in a few words on each index card.

6 Associate each mental cue with a location in your Memory Palace, in order. Convert specific details like sales data or other numbers using one of the number systems in this book. Give details their own locations so you're sure to remember them.

7 Mentally walk through your Memory Palace, adding details to your mental images with CAST (**C**olor, **A**ction, **S**ize, and **T**exture). Make them silly and interesting to make them memorable.

8 Stand up and practice your speech out loud, mentally walking through each location and seeing the images of your main points. If one or two aren't instantly memorable, fix them by repeating step 5. How bizarre can you make the image? That's what you're going for.

9 Continue practicing out loud, standing up, and without notes. Make your mind recall the silly images from each location. Relying on your memory in practice will help you tremendously later.

This method is quite different from what you may be familiar with, but I encourage you to try it. The small learning curve is worth the effort because it is so powerful to deliver a speech or presentation from memory. People are very impressed with those who can do it. Once you practice this method, you'll see how easy it really is.

[56] Remember Unique Passwords for Online Security

YOU MUST HAVE a different, completely unique password for every log-in. Period. Cybersecurity experts also recommend that each password be at least twelve characters long. Sixteen is better. How can you remember so many long passwords? "My browser remembers and fills them in for me." But what happens if your computer is lost, stolen, broken, or you otherwise need to log in from a computer other than your own? Trouble! Many people use password management software, but several popular password managers have had major security flaws.

There are ample reasons to use the greatest password manager of all: your memory. This hack makes it simple to be secure.

THE TECHNIQUE ⦙ Picturing the Anchor

I wrote an entire book about creating your own system for remembering passwords (*The Hack-Proof Password System*), but this section summarizes several of the main strategies. If cybersecurity is essential in your career, workplace, or industry, though, I encourage you to read the whole book.

The biggest problem with forgetting passwords is that people forget to anchor the log-in site to the password. You may remember that one of your passwords is 5V8k22/>19dpb but forget that it's for the credit card account you rarely access. To remember passwords, always start by creatively changing the site into an image to use as the anchor.

HOW TO DO IT ⟩

1 Start with the anchor. To picture the website, think of what the company or page reminds you of. If you have to log in to Grandpa's House of Fish Food, picture the logo of Grandpa, your favorite fish, or an aquarium. Be obvious in your anchor image choice, not clever. You need to be able to recall the anchor even if you haven't visited the website in months.

2 Do you receive random passwords to memorize, like 8,b[X-Y,B/Q,ekQg? If so, use one of the number

memorization systems, such as Alphabet Images (see page 24), and creatively convert commas, dashes, and other characters into pictures. For example, a comma could be a snail and a slash could be a children's slide. Then link them together by associating them with each other using the Chain Method (see page 78). Repeat, adding details.

3 When you create your own password, select words that link together, following these steps:

   a] Create an image of the site as your anchor. Ask yourself what the anchor most reminds you of and picture it.

   b] The next link in the chain is a word that reminds you of the anchor image. Picture that and connect it to the anchor image.

   c] What does that link remind you of? Choose a word and picture that as the next link. Connect them creatively.

   d] Keep going until you have at least three words and twelve letters.

   e] Repeat the process, adding details to the images.

   f] As soon as you log in to the site with your new password, immediately log off, then back on. Do this three times in a row so you're typing and mentally reviewing your new password each time.

Here's an example:

Grandpa's House of Fish Food Website

> *Anchor: Your grandpa or Grandpa's image from the website. What does Grandpa remind you of? My grandpa had huge ears, so the first word link in the chain could be "hugeears." Add details as you picture Grandpa first and then the rest of the chain.*

What do huge ears remind me of? Huge head-
phones: "headphones." Huge ears are easy to
mentally associate with headphones.

We need a few more letters. Headphones remind
me of my favorite band: Room101. I can easily con-
nect headphones with room101.

The entire password: hugeearsheadphonesroom101. Are there issues
with this password? Yes. It would be better to have at least one capital
letter and one symbol. Having a number at the end is very common and
makes it easier to hack. See the tip to improve this.

TIP | SUBSTITUTE SYMBOLS

Develop your own password system with rules
that includes letters you substitute a symbol for
(not @ for "a" or any of the other obvious ones),
which letters you substitute a number for (don't
use 5 for "s"), and which words or letters you will
always capitalize. Pick up my password book,
The Hack-Proof Password System, for an easy
guide through this process to make sure you're
secure online.

[57] Remember Instructions
from a Manager or Boss

THE BIGGEST CAUSE of a poor memory problem at work is
multitasking. Trying to get too much done at once invariably leads to
memory issues, because we aren't bringing our entire focus to one issue
at a time. That's why it's often hard to remember what our manager tells
us. How do you listen attentively while still getting all your work done?
You need to tell the task you're working on that you'll BRB ("be right
back") and turn your attention to your manager.

This is like the CARE Method for remembering people's details (page 40), but I've modified it for the work environment. BRB brings your attention to where it belongs (your manager) and lets you focus on them, remember what they say, and then get back to your previous task. BRB stands for:

- **B**reathe
- **R**epeat
- **B**ring to mind

Let's see how this can be used to never again forget something important you're told at work.

HOW TO DO IT ⟩

1   When your boss needs to tell you something, think BRB. *Breathe* in and out once, drawing your focus away from what you had been doing and toward your boss. If possible, physically break your current attention by turning toward them. If they're calling you, look at the phone on your desk.

2   *Repeat* a keyword or phrase that your boss says. This is another trick to bring your focus to what is being said.

3   *Bring to mind* an image of what your boss wants or has said. Imagine yourself doing or finishing the task. The more details you can visualize, the sharper it will be in your mind.

Here's an example:

> *You're working on your TPS report when your boss walks by your cubicle. "Oh," she says, "I need you to do something for me." Think "BRB" and turn away from the computer and look at her.*
>
> *Breathe in and out, focusing your attention on your boss as you do so. Listen as she tells you about the other big thing she needs done. Repeat, "Okay, you need the Penske file by the end of the day." Picture Mr. Penske, the company logo, or turn the name*

into an image (a pen skiing). Remember that silly, strange, or funny images are easier to remember. Repeat as needed based on what else she says.

Before returning to your previous task, make a mental note, reviewing the conversation. To add a mental reminder of a certain date or time, read Master Due Dates of Assignments and Deadlines on page 128.

Completing the BRB steps before returning to your previous work will help your mind keep track of what you're told and remember what to do when you finish your current task.

[58] Master Due Dates of Assignments and Deadlines

IF IT'S IMPORTANT, write it down! I'm a big fan of red marks on calendars and sticky note reminders for essential projects. Does that sound strange coming from a memory improvement expert? I believe that if forgetting something may have huge repercussions, it should be remembered *and* written down. Sometimes life happens and we forget no matter how hard we try or what technique we use.

After you've marked your calendar or written your sticky note, though, get busy making sure you remember it. Make your memory the primary system and your calendar a backup system.

THE TECHNIQUE ⦂ Envision the Day or Date

This is a straightforward method that requires a small upfront investment—or being very creative in the moment. It's similar to the technique for remembering birthdays (see page 42) but uses a different anchor image: the name of the assignment, the person, client, or department that it's for.

You'll use the Month Memorization System (see page 27) or the Days of the Week System (see page 98) to keep track of the day. Adding the date is simple if you use one of the number systems. Connecting them together with the image of the assignment and adding creative details will keep it in your mind, especially as the deadline approaches.

HOW TO DO IT >

1   Create an image of the assignment by converting the name of the client or project into an image.

2   Use one of the systems from earlier in the book (or your creativity) to imagine the month, date, or day of the deadline.

3   Connect the assignment image and the deadline image. Make it creative and strange.

4   Review and add details.

5   Whenever you work on the assignment, think of the deadline and picture the odd image or movie.

Here are two examples:

The Denman file is due March 23.

1   Image ideas for Denman: den = a bear's den. Picture a half-bear, half-man creature.

2   March = *march*ing, a leprechaun, or St. Patrick's Day. 23 = Michael Jordan's jersey number.

3   Picture a half bear-half man marching in a St. Patrick's Day parade with Michael Jordan, passing a basketball back and forth as they go.

Your report is due on February 11, but there are other deadlines along the way.

January 3   Part 1 due

January 16   Part 2 due

| January 28 | Part 3 due |
| February 11 | Completed document due |

1 Picture the bound report. Make up a cover page that is over-the-top with gold embossed letters, a beautiful binding, and thick, expensive paper. Or go the other direction and make it horribly ugly, plaid, tie-dye, or fluorescent green.

2 January = Baby New Year. 3 = tricycle.

3 Picture Baby New Year riding a tricycle over your report, which isn't hard because it's looking pretty thin with only the first part done.

4 Repeat for part 2. 16 = the age many people get a driver's license. See Baby New Year now driving a car over your report, hitting it like a minor speed bump. If you need more for "part 2" think of a pair of shoes for "2" and see the car driving over the shoes.

5 Repeat for part 3. 28 = shoes (2) on an octopus (8). Baby New Year and an octopus wearing two shoes wrestle with your now quite thick report that has a picture of a tricycle on the cover to represent 3.

Use this technique to keep your mind sharp and impress people at the office. Instead of looking up the deadline for each project, you'll know it "off the top of your head." I can't overstate how amazed people are with the ability to remember details like this.

[59] The Next Level: Remember More Names for Business

IF YOUR LIVELIHOOD depends on how well you know the names of prospects, clients, and coworkers, it's time to step up your game and master memorizing names. The Ask a Question technique detailed in part 1 on page 11 is an excellent first step, but it may not be enough. There are two others that will take your memory for names to the next level.

The Facial Feature Method relies on being able to identify and remember facial features well. This has always been hard for me as I have a mild form of face blindness (prosopagnosia), the inability to recognize faces. However, if you're a person who "never forgets a face," this technique may work well for you. The Best Friend Method is easier for me because it starts with the name and then connects the face. This often works well for people who are introverts or "word people."

Both hacks make names memorable by associating them with something you already know. Try both and use the one that works best for you. You can also practice both techniques and use whichever one appeals to you more when you meet a new person.

HOW TO DO IT >

THE FACIAL FEATURE METHOD

This technique works well when someone's face is memorable.

1 Identify an obvious facial feature that stands out: amazingly beautiful eyes, a unique nose, sharp cheekbones, big dimples, etc.

2 Use the Ask a Question (page 11) technique to hear the person's name and cement it in your short-term memory.

3 Change the name into a picture like with the CAR Method for learning foreign languages (see page 71).

4 Associate the picture with the person's unique facial feature.

5 Review the facial feature, their name, and the creative connection after you finish speaking with them, and again later that day when you brush your teeth.

6 Repeat the review the following morning and again later the next night.

Here's an example:

> *You meet a man with a noticeably long nose named Tony. You identify the nose, discuss his name ("Is that short for Anthony?"), and change the name into a picture of a toe. Imagine a large toe instead of his nose.*

THE BEST FRIEND TECHNIQUE

This technique works well for most people.

1 Learn someone's name. Use the Ask a Question technique (see page 11).

2 While discussing the name, think of someone else who shares the name, like a famous person or a friend of yours.

3 Mentally compare the person you've met with the famous person or your friend. What features are similar and what are different? Are they complete opposites? Study the person, looking for a resemblance.

4 Review the interesting interactions that night, the next morning, and again as needed.

Here's an example:

> *You meet a person named Larry ("Is that short for Lawrence or just Larry?"). The person you've met is about 5'9", with dark curly hair, and solidly built like a football player. You compare him to your friend named Larry (if you have one), the basketball player Larry Bird, or the comedian Larry David.*
>
> *Note the differences and similarities as you chat. Imagine him playing one-on-one basketball with 6'9" Larry Bird. Picture him onstage telling jokes with Larry David. Add exaggerated details: Is new Larry so excited to meet Larry Bird that he starts to cry? Is new Larry better at basketball?*

To use this technique with the Tony in the first example I'd imagine him interacting with Tony Soprano, Tony Stark, Tony Shalhoub—or all three!

Regardless of the technique you use, the three keys to maximizing your memory for names are: 1) If you miss the person's name, apologize and immediately ask for it again (it's much better to admit you missed it than to have to ask again days later); 2) Frequently review the names of the people you meet; and 3) Make the decision that people's names truly matter to you. This tells your mind to pay attention, and it will work harder to help you.

[60] Remember Names for Networking

IN BUSINESS—ESPECIALLY sales—we often meet people at trade shows, mixers, or other networking events. Knowing the names of people is an essential tool in work and sales, but the ability to introduce people is a skill that really impresses. Not only do people appreciate hearing their name and knowing someone remembers them, they love it when they're introduced to other people. You'll be a networking pro and prized for your genius-level memory skills.

THE TECHNIQUE : The Introduction Method

Introducing people to others requires that you remember the name in the first place. Use the Facial Feature or Best Friend Method (see page 131) to start the process. As soon as possible after learning the new person's name, introduce them to someone else. As you introduce them, be sure to make use of the Ask a Question technique (see page 11). Mention what you learned—their name is short for the common longer version (Tom but short for Thomas, for example) or the spelling. If applicable, you can also add, "This is Brad . . . like Brad Pitt!"

Once you start practicing this technique, your memory for names will go into overdrive. Your mind recognizes that it will be called on immediately, so your focus improves.

1   As you introduce the person, visualize the mental connection you made when you met them. Saying their name again tells your mind this is especially important, and reviewing the silly image helps even more.

2   Take breaks from meeting people every 5, 10, or 15 minutes, depending on your capacity for new names, your skill level, and the natural ebb and flow of the event. Excuse yourself to go to the buffet, get something to drink, or check your phone. Then mentally review the faces and the names of the people you've met. If possible, locate them around the room and reassociate their face with your mental image of their name. Adding a minute of review will greatly add to your recall later.

3   Combine this technique with the next technique to remember details about people, and then share a pertinent detail or two when you introduce that person to someone else. It's a great conversation starter and will solidify the name and details into your mind. You'll soon have a valuable reputation as someone who "knows everybody"!

[61] Remember Details of Clients, Prospects, and Coworkers

BUILDING CONNECTIONS AND instilling trust is tremendously important in life and business. How can we do that, though, if we frequently forget people's details? A salesperson I worked with often lost sales because of his memory. One prospect told him, "I'm not at all interested in ABC because . . ." but 10 minutes later, my colleague was explaining the benefits of ABC. The expression on the prospect's face: confusion followed by disappointment and lack of trust. He probably thought, "How can I trust this guy to help me find the right product when he clearly doesn't listen?"

Improving your listening skills and memory will result in easier connections, better likability, and more business.

The technique is a modification of the CARE Method you learned on page 40. It's a simple method of remembering details about the lives and preferences of your coworkers, clients, or prospects. Here, we add an *s* to CARE:

- **C**ommit
- Pay **A**ttention
- **R**epeat
- **E**nvision
- **S**hare

Sharing works especially well in business and sales.

1   **COMMIT.** Many people are able to commit to being a better listener in the work environment than at home with their family. Still, be sure to commit to listening with intention. Go into the encounter with the goal of listening to what the other person says and how they say it.

2   **PAY ATTENTION.** It's important to listen with your full attention without thinking about or planning what you will say next. Watch the face and body language of the other person. Stay focused by noting their attitude, expressions, and moods.

3   **REPEAT.** Listen for key details such as likes and dislikes, names of important people in their lives, hobbies, and interests. The details will vary depending on what type of conversation you are having, but if you're listening, you will know the right details when you hear them. Repeat a keyword or phrase as appropriate. "Oh, you hate the color blue?"

4   ENVISION. Translate the keyword or phrase into a picture and envision them doing it. Visualize them smashing the product you were going to suggest with a hammer because they said they had one previously they didn't like. Imagine the person and their golden retriever out for a walk. Picture them and their three kids playing together.

5   SHARE. Briefly share a detail that relates to theirs and end with a question. "I love dogs and have one of my own. How old is yours?" or "Blue is our most popular color, but we have it in others. What is your favorite color?"

6   GO BACK TO STEP ONE AND REPEAT THE PROCESS. There will be a natural break where it's your turn to talk about yourself, business, or your products. Until then, commit to listening and learning about your prospect, client, or coworker.

7   AFTER THE CONVERSATION REVIEW THE KEY DETAILS USING AS MUCH CREATIVITY AS POSSIBLE. Try to imagine how the dog looks or what their kids are like. This review tells your mind the details are important. Visualizing them is the way to help your mind remember best.

8   WHEN YOU NEXT SEE THE PERSON YOU'LL NATURALLY REMEMBER THE CONVERSATION AND THE DETAILS WILL POP INTO YOUR MIND. You can start the conversation with a question like, "Hey, how's your dog?" or "Last time we spoke I think you mentioned you had three kids—is that right? How are they?" They'll appreciate how much you care and be impressed by your memory and listening skills.

[62] Remember the Lunch or Coffee Order at Work

"HEY, PICK ME up a latte on the way back, will you?" Do you have to grab a pen and sticky note to remember your coworker's order? By using your imagination, you'll impress everyone as you remember how they like their coffee or their lunch order without using notes. If you learn and use this method people will think you're a genius!

Once again, remembering the difficult becomes easy if you use your powers of imagination and association. You will picture the person, exaggerating them to make them more memorable, and then picture their order. That means translating anything not easily recalled into an interesting image. Then you'll connect the person with the order. It's the Link Method (see page 67) modified for food and drink, though it can also be used to remember to pick up dry-cleaning, toner for the printer, or any other order you're asked to handle.

HOW TO DO IT

1 Pick a feature of the person for whom you're getting the coffee, food, or other item.

2 Translate the order into another creative mental image. It should be easy to remember coffee, for example, but what about the other details? Add as many silly details as needed to fix it in your mind:

   - Picture the size by exaggerating: a one-ounce cup of coffee for small, five-gallon bucket for medium, and a hot tub for large.
   - A latte could be a fancy watch (the word "latte" looks like "late"). An iced coffee can be imagined as a huge block of dry ice.
   - Any other details can also easily be imagined (including soy milk: picture a block of soy tofu instead of the milk).

3 Many times people will say, "Everything except . . ." and list an item or two. For example, "I'll have a BLT on wheat with everything, but make sure they don't put mayo or butter on it." What then? To exclude something, you still picture it (so you don't remember what not to include) but think of it being destroyed, left behind, locked up, or otherwise prevented from being added.

Here's an example:

You picture your manager and a BLT (a pig wrapped in lettuce with a tomato in its mouth) in a field of wheat (make sure the pig image is huge so it's easy to see in that field). Picture standing near the pig, valiantly defending it from the huge jar of mayonnaise approaching. In the other direction, a stick of butter is sneaking up. You turn back and forth, intent on not letting either one get near.

This is an easy way to make a big impact at work. Most people feel overwhelmed with taking someone's coffee or food order, let alone having to remember to stop at the office store and pick up several items. Using this technique takes little effort and greatly impresses people. It's your call: Help them out by teaching it to them, or keep it to yourself and let them assume you're brilliant.

[63] Remember Customers' Favorite Orders & Preferences

DO YOU HAVE a favorite coffee shop, restaurant, or vendor? Chances are, they've made the effort to know what you like, and you feel valued when they remember it. We can do the same with our customers and clients by using memory hacks to remember what they prefer. The more they feel important and special, the more business they bring.

It doesn't have to be daunting. We naturally remember these important details—in time, through rote memorization. Someone ordering a certain item every week will eventually stick in our minds. But by consciously applying this memory technique we can make the process easier and quicker.

THE TECHNIQUE · Recognize and Associate

This is the CAR Method (see page 71) with a twist. You have to remember your client somehow. Review The Next Level: Remember More Names for Business on page 130 for strategies to remember what and who they look like. Next, you convert their favorite order into an image. That should be pretty simple whether it's a preferred service, an inventory item, or even something intangible like a stock or mutual fund. Associate the customer with the image of their preference, and then add details while reviewing.

HOW TO DO IT >

1 Convert the customer into an image. Use their name, see their face, or imagine their company name or logo.

2 Convert the preference into an image. Make it interesting and exaggerated.

3 Associate the customer and the preference in a unique, strange, or silly way.

4 Review the connection. Can you make it bigger, more colorful, add more action, emotion, or texture? The mental story or movie should be vivid and clear.

Here's an example:

> *Ted doesn't use computers much but loves technology investments. As his financial adviser, you talk to him monthly about his portfolio, and he's always looking for ideas about tech stocks. While this should be easy to remember, for some reason you have a hard time keeping it in mind. Drive your CAR to the rescue.*

1 What does Ted remind you of? Is he a voice on the phone or do you know him well? Picture him in your mind.

2 When you think of technology investments, what is the first thing that comes to mind? Can you boil it down to an icon, like a computer? Imagine the computer, including color and shape. Don't make it sleek and cool: Imagine an old fashioned, huge, dated computer. Don't worry, you won't think, "Oh, Ted likes to invest in old-fashioned things." Imagining something outdated, ugly, or broken is often more memorable than something modern and gorgeous.

3   Associate Ted with the computer image. He's juggling several computers, drooling over how cool they are, collecting them and stacking them up, or whatever your mind creates.

4   Review, adding detail and especially more emotion.

You can do the same for a customer's coffee order by imagining their face with their favorite drink variations balanced on their head: *Caffè Marocchino a la Italia* could be pressing (espresso) melted chocolate (the image for the cocoa powder) into their hair and adding a bunch of milk froth in a swirl to their eyebrows. The next time you see them, your mind will recall the creative image, especially if you add more details.

[64] Recognize Voices on the Phone

A CALL COMES in. The voice greets you by name and starts chattering away about a business topic as you rack your brain to figure out who it could be. They know you, but you can't place them. Sometimes we recognize the voice but can't recall the person's name or company. If this happens occasionally, people are sure to understand. If it happens often, it becomes an embarrassing liability. Can you identify your favorite singer's voice even if it's a new song or the voice of an actor without seeing the TV? If so, you can improve your auditory memory, too.

THE TECHNIQUE : Identify Vocal Characteristics

The first step in this process is to assess whether you are having trouble identifying voices or if it's difficult to connect the voice with a specific person's name and details. The next steps are to be able to identify a person and to create a mental identifier for their voice. To better recognize voices, it helps to draw your attention to how different people sound. Start with your family and coworkers and get into the habit of noticing these vocal characteristics:

- **AGE.** How old do they sound?
- **LEVEL.** Are they quiet or loud?
- **SPEED.** How quickly do they speak?

- **TONE AND EMOTION.** What is their normal, everyday emotion or tone?
- **UNIQUE.** Do you hear a texture or quality that is rare?
- **VOCABULARY.** What type of words do they normally choose?
- **WEIGHT.** Does their voice sound light or heavy?

Notice voices in your daily interactions and identify the characteristics of different people's voices. Your mind will develop the ability to better recognize the people you speak with so you can move on to the next steps of connecting them with their personal details.

HOW TO DO IT

1 Identify the clients whose voices you have trouble remembering or connecting to a name. Consider the characteristics of the way they speak listed earlier. With voices, we develop a mental image that isn't visual—it's more of a sense or feeling. We "know" a voice by identifying its characteristics, so create a mental "feeling" for them. Mentally hear their voices.

2 Convert their name into a picture. Use the Best Friend Method (see page 131): Think of a famous person or friend with the same name and picture them in your mind.

3 Associate the picture with the sound of them speaking.

4 Think of the client's business matters and any pertinent information you need to remember. (See "Remember Customers' Favorite Orders & Preferences" on page 138 for more.) Convert the information into mental images.

5 Connect their name with the information in a memorable, creative way. Connect the client details with the mental image and the mental "feeling" you have of them. You're making a chain of connections for your mind to follow.

When you recognize the voice or hear the name and recall what it reminds you of, your mind will follow the pathway to the details you need. The majority of the results come from making the effort to identify the voices and names of your customers. Things quickly fall into place once you communicate to your mind—through your daily efforts—that this is a priority for you.

[65] Fix "It's on the Tip of My Tongue" Syndrome

REMEMBER THAT THERE are three essential steps to memory: Focus on the information, arrange the material in the mind, and retrieve it from your mind when you need it (FAR). Many people find themselves tripped up by the last step. It's common, especially as we age, to have trouble accessing information as quickly as we'd like. This often leads to a frustrating "It's on the tip of my tongue" moment; the memory is *right there*, but for some reason you can't quite access it.

THE TECHNIQUE : The Topic and Alphabet Access Methods

There are several hacks for this phenomenon. Getting more sleep is a great place to start. A well-rested mind is more alert, nimble, and functional. It's also important to relax. A mind under pressure or stress has more trouble accessing stored memory than a calm, serene mind. If you frequently suffer from this syndrome, you'll love these two helpful techniques:

> **THE TOPIC METHOD:** As soon as you realize you're blanking out on something you know, start naming other things you can think of that are similar.

> **THE ALPHABET ACCESS METHOD:** Some people prefer this because it has more structure. Start with "A" and list things that are similar to what you are trying to recall, letter by letter.

HOW TO DO IT

TOPIC METHOD

1 You realize you know something but can't quite recall it.

2 List other similar items in your mind until you arrive at the word you are looking for.

Here's an example:

> *Someone you know relatively well is walking toward you, but his name has fled your mind. You know* him and his name, *but your mind isn't doing its job.*

> *Start thinking of names in your mind: Ron, Rocco, Jim, Dana, John, Joe, Robb, Max... You're telling your mind, "What you're looking for is like one of these things. What is it?" Your memory detective will know what to look for and provide you with the answer.*

1 You realize you know something but can't quite recall it.

2 List other similar items in your mind starting with the letter "A" and continuing through the alphabet until you remember it.

Here's an example:

> *You can't remember the name of the movie you watched last week. Start naming movies by letter:* "Apollo 13. Braveheart. Cars. Dances with Wolves. East of Eden... *The process of forcing your mind to find other similar information, especially by a specific letter, often jogs the memory quickly.*

Try both methods and see which one works best for you. My coaching clients often have strong preferences; what works best for one person may not work at all for another. Be constructive: Either technique is better than complaining that you can't remember! The main ways I avoid this syndrome are taking care of my mind and using memory hacks to remember information. When we encode information in fun, creative ways, it is much easier to recall later. But for those times when the mind doesn't seem to want to play along, one of these two techniques will help.

[66] Remember Emergency Procedures

DO YOU REMEMBER your workplace safety plan? Do you know the two closest evacuation routes in the event of an emergency? Do you remember where the fire extinguishers are located? Trying to remember what you're supposed to do when under pressure is difficult. Trying to remember without ever learning it is impossible.

This may be an uncomfortable subject to consider, but it's important. By applying a memory hack, in addition to practice and review, you may feel more secure and be prepared in the event of a dangerous situation.

THE TECHNIQUE : Learn and Focus

The main focus of this hack is: Focus! Simply drawing your attention to a number of important safety matters will get your mind started on the path to remembering. Using your imagination will be another step toward easy recall in the event of an emergency. Finally, reviewing the plan using spaced repetition and a reminder system will help prepare your mind for something everyone hopes will never be needed.

HOW TO DO IT

1   What is the evacuation plan for your office? If it's written, find it. If it's not, write your own.

2   Review the evacuation plan, noting the nearest exits as well as alternative exits that could be used in an emergency, like windows or doors that are farther away.

3   Arrive before work or take time during a lunch break to walk the routes, including using the alternate exits.

4   Mentally review each evacuation path by visualizing yourself using them calmly but quickly. See yourself turning the door handle or pushing the bar for the door. Do not imagine any specific emergency or induce panic in your mental imagery; simply picture yourself exiting safely.

5 Find the location of the fire extinguishers in the areas you most frequent. Visualize the areas as flashing with bright red strobe lights. Mentally walk around your area counting the fire extinguishers until you can go forward and backward, listing at least the nearest three.

6 Repeat step 5 with the locations of the fire alarms. They may (or may not) be near the fire extinguishers.

7 Look for locations for concealment—hiding yourself—and cover, which is a location that would possibly stop a bullet. Mentally walk to those areas and imagine yourself hiding. Imagine yourself being calm, cool, and collected.

8 Think of any coworkers who may need help in the event of an emergency. Imagine how you could get to their workspace if necessary, how you would evacuate from their area or hide near them.

9 Review all the information in steps 1 though 8 three times at the end of the workday and again three times tomorrow.

10 On the first of each month, review your emergency procedures. Remember this by thinking "safety first" for the *first* of every month.

[67] Impress with Your Memory for Product and Service Prices

WHETHER YOU'RE BUYING or selling, remembering the cost of items can be a big time-saver. It can also help you stand out from the pack at work—in a good or bad way, depending on how well or poorly you remember. If you know every price in the catalog or on the menu people will notice and be impressed. The good news is that it's not difficult and can even be fun.

THE TECHNIQUE • Link Items and Numbers

To remember the prices of items, you will translate numbers into images and link them to an image of the product. Translating numbers into images means you must have a solid foundation with one of the number systems presented earlier in the book.

I recommend the Major System (see page 35) as it is the most robust and best for large amounts of numbers. "But that's a lot of work," some people say. So is learning to drive instead of walking, but if we want to get somewhere quickly, it's easier to learn to drive than to walk. If your job performance or efficiency depends on knowing a lot of prices, it makes sense to learn a system that will help you for the rest of your career.

HOW TO DO IT

1　Learn a number system like the Major System. However, depending on your industry and the amount you need to memorize, it may be enough to use the MOST Method of converting numbers into money amounts, objects, sports scores, or time (see page 22).

2　Convert any product into an image. This can be challenging if the product is a certain-size ball bearing, a computer chip, or a service, but anything can be imagined with enough creativity. In a pinch, simply assign an image to the product. For example, if there are five variations of a product and you can't think of another way to translate them into pictures, choose items like a ping-pong ball, baseball, softball, basketball, and a football. Also designating products as red, blue, yellow, and green allows you to associate the color with fruits and vegetables.

3　Link the item and the number images together by creating a story. Be as wild and interesting as you can be. Here's an example:

> Your work at Big Box TV and Computers requires constant customer interaction with many asking, "How much is this one?" You need to remember pricing for the top products like the price of the most popular TV:
>
> Brand "I" 65-inch 4K TV Sale: $519.99 (normally $599.99)

Your memory detective will help you remember many of the details—like how your store always prices items so they end in ".99," and all the TVs you offer are 4K—so all you need to memorize is "Brand I" and the price, including the sale price.

"Brand I" could be pictured as an "eye." Imagine "sale" by picturing a huge red sale sign, and put an image of a huge eyeball on it. Make the whites of the eyeball bloodshot to match the sign.

Convert 519 into an image. The first thing that comes to me is running a 5 minute, 19 second mile. Combine them together: I run a 5:19 mile, crossing the finish line tape, which is a giant sale sign banner with a huge eyeball on it, and then I'm awarded a TV for winning the race. To add the 599 normal price, think of what 599 (or 600 minus one) reminds you of. Or translate 599 into an image using the MOST Method: Your child's basketball team plays against a pro team and loses 5 to 99 while you watch on the big TV at work.

Using the Simple System (page 25), 519 could also be pictured as a fisherman (5) waving a baseball bat (1) to try to keep a cat (9) away from his fish.

4   Select 5 to 10 items per day and learn them well before moving on to the next set. Review daily until you can instantly see the image associations between the price and the product. Make a game out of it by challenging your coworkers to see who can remember better or who can create the most memorable mental images.

[68] Remember What's in Inventory

"DO YOU HAVE this in stock?" . . . "Hold on, let me check." It's easy enough to check the inventory, but wouldn't it be more impressive and better customer service to just know what you have? "That's impossible," you say? It's not! You can do it, and it's amazingly simple.

It may not be practical for all industries, but knowing if you have three or ten cars, 88-inch TVs, or wind turbines immediately available is something you can do to amaze clients (and managers).

THE TECHNIQUE ⦙ The CAR Method with Frequent Review

This is the CAR Method (see page 71) with frequent updates. You'll imagine the inventory item, which should be easy to translate into an image. Next, you'll translate the number of items into a picture using one of the number systems. By associating them in a creative way and then reviewing with added details, you'll have it.

When it's time to recall the number in inventory, you will picture the object and immediately think of the image associated with it. This will give you the number of items on hand. What about when that number changes? Read on.

HOW TO DO IT

1 Review your inventory on a regular basis.

2 Create an image for the first inventory item you want to keep track of.

3 Create an image for the number of items in stock. Use Rhyme Time (see page 33) or the Simple System (see page 25) if you typically have fewer than nine items, the Major System (see page 35) or the MOST Method (see page 22) if you usually carry more.

4 Associate the item and number together. Be creative.

5 Review, adding details. Exaggerate.

6 When the amount in your inventory changes, you need to change the number image. Before you connect the new number with the object, destroy the previous story or movie of the item and number. Ways to do that include imagining the number image damaged or removed from the story: Crush, ruin, harm, or otherwise destroy it in a way that makes it clear that it is no longer the correct image for the number of objects in inventory.

7 Reconnect the item with the new amount.

Here's an example:

> *You have nine Superfast cars in stock. You can picture the Superfast model because you love it. The tail, the hood, the headlamps. Zoom. Nine can be remembered by nine lives—a cat. Make your cat interesting by seeing its green and pink fur. Picture a Superfast car with a cat sharpening its claws on the hood, ruining the glorious paint. See yourself out in the lot, desperately trying to fix the claw marks.*
>
> *On Monday afternoon, you and your coworker sell three cars. Imagine taking the cat home to your family, thereby destroying the original idea of having nine cars in inventory. With six cars left, you see that you've accidentally parked the demo car on top of an ant (6) hill and the interior is swarming with biting red ants.*
>
> *It would be an extra (easy) step to know that there are two red cars, two black ones, and two yellow. Apply your own ideas to how you could do this to kick things up a notch.*

[69] Remember Phone Numbers

DON'T SKIP THIS hack! To call people these days we click speed dial, tell our device to place the call, or dial the number from a customer relationship management system. But there are excellent reasons to remember phone numbers instead of relying on technology:

- It's an easy way to stay mentally fit and exercise your memory. This is the mental equivalent to walking up a flight of stairs instead of taking the elevator.
- Knowing a prospect or client's phone number impresses them.
- It's more efficient.

- Sometimes technology fails us at the worst possible moment.
- In case of emergencies.

Don't get me wrong, I'm not advocating memorizing every phone number you may use. Here are some important ones to know:

- Your number one client's main and secondary numbers. Impress him by being able to say, "Should I call you on the 9534 number or your 2579 cell?"
- Top business professionals like your attorney, primary care physician, financial planner, and accountant.
- Professionals like your veterinarian, child's school, child's doctor, and dentist.
- All immediate family members, plus a favorite neighbor who can help out in a pinch.
- Also important are the local police nonemergency contact number, poison control, place of worship, and top two babysitters if you have kids.

Don't worry—you've had experience with numbers elsewhere in the book, so this should be easy. Keep in mind that once upon a time people routinely memorized phone numbers!

HOW TO DO IT

1 Pick an essential phone number.

2 Imagine the person as your anchor image.

3 If necessary, translate the three-digit area code into an image. If you know the area code once you're reminded it may be enough to translate 518, for example, into a fisherman (for 5, which looks like a fishhook. See the Simple System on page 25).

   If the area code isn't familiar to you even with a reminder, convert each digit into an image using one of the number systems. Picture the anchor image (the person) and create a story using each digit. For example, for your attorney's number in area code 518, imagine your attorney (anchor) fishing (5), reeling in a baseball bat (1), when an octopus (8) reaches out and grabs it (the numbers in this example are from the Simple System).

4   Continue the story using the Chain Method (see page 78) to connect each link to the next.

5   Review and add details.

6   Use your phone's keypad to pretend to dial the number from memory as you recall the exaggerated links you created. This puts your memory to work and adds a physical dimension to it, which helps your mind.

7   Review the phone number images tonight and again tomorrow morning when you brush your teeth.

Here's an example:

> Here's the phone number for the White House (please don't bother them needlessly!): (202) 456-1111.
>
> For your anchor, imagine the current president, your favorite president, or the White House itself. I'll use the President and use Rhyme Time (page 33) as the number system.
>
> Imagine the President in the Oval Office putting on shoes (2) alongside your favorite superhero (0), who is also putting on their shoes (2).
>
> Next connect the shoes (2) to a door (4). Imagine the superhero's shoes kicking open a door only to encounter a beehive (5). The bees have sticks (6) and go on a rampage having fun (1) hitting four different, specific things in the scenario, like the Resolute desk, a painting, a couch, and the drapes.
>
> Add details, then pretend to call the White House on your phone's keypad to solidify the movie in your mind.

[70] Keep Track of What You've Assigned and When It's Due

AN OUTSTANDING TEAM is essential for success in business. Managing a team well takes many skills, among them being able to keep track of who is doing what work and the deadlines associated with it. Remembering your own work plus that of others is added strain on your mind. Memory hacks can help make the process easier and less stressful.

THE TECHNIQUE : The Mega Method

There are two small but powerful methods I often use independently. When they are combined, they create the Mega Method. The first method is Mind Mapping (see page 63). It allows for a visual reference to how much is assigned to each person or team. A version of the Chain Method (see page 78) is the second way to remember what has been assigned and the associated deadlines.

Starting with the Mind Map is often enough to visualize and remember the details. When there are several deadlines or other parts, I add the Chain Method. When combined, this Mega Method makes it easy to remember what each person or team is doing.

HOW TO DO IT

MIND MAPPING

1   Use a piece of paper (not a computer) to Mind Map each team member's responsibilities. Start with the name of the person in the center of the page.

2   Write the biggest or most important assignment in large letters using red ink with a thick circle around it. Add lines branching away with details like the deadlines, resources, and any other important details using different colored inks. Surround each with different shapes.

3   Continue with other tasks using different-size writing, colors, and thinner lines.

4   Look at the masterpiece you've created (don't worry if it's gorgeous or ugly—both are memorable), and then close

your eyes. Test yourself to remember the layout, colors, lines, and shapes. Repeat until you have a mental image of the important details.

5   If the situation is complex, continue to the Chain Method to remember everything.

THE CHAIN METHOD

1   Start with the image of the person as your anchor.

2   Convert the first item to remember (like the project name or the first assignment) into an image.

3   Connect that detail to the anchor image of the person.

4   Convert other details (deadlines, resources) into images and attach them to the previous image like links in a chain.

5   Use a chain for each important assignment.

6   Then, to remember the many assignment chains for each person, make the anchor image itself into a memorable movie. Here's an example:

> *Brad has a book to write, a presentation to customize, and a student to coach. Create an anchor image of Brad doing all three things so you can follow each chain. See Brad frantically typing on his laptop held in one hand and writing on a projector screen with the other hand while blowing a whistle to motivate the student in front of him. In this way you can review what you've assigned to Brad by imagining his face, and the image of him working on all three tasks will pop into your mind.*

7   Follow each mental chain: The laptop is held by Cupid (February) who is playfully tapping Brad with two baseball bats (1,1) signifying that the book deadline is February 11. The presentation screen marches away wearing two huge boots (March 2) as Brad tries to write on it, showing the deadline for the presentation is March 2.

[71] Advanced: Project Management

THIS IS AN advanced brain hack that takes some effort. If you are involved in project management and want to excel or impress, however, you'll find this very useful. There is a lot to be said for the ability to hold a huge amount of material in your mind—like all the details of a complex project. It gives you a grasp on the structure, the potential issues and bottlenecks, and absolutely stuns other people.

THE TECHNIQUE ⦂ Per Project Memory Palaces

This technique takes about 10 to 20 minutes of upfront effort and then another 20 to 50 minutes to commit the project to memory. One of the biggest complaints from people exposed to memory hacks is, "That's harder than just doing it 'normally'!" If by "normally" people mean "easily forgetting, making excuses, and apologizing," I completely agree. Yes, this memory hack takes upfront effort, but it's easy. It's just different. And to many people, different feels uncomfortable. But you're reading this for a reason, so give it a try.

If you haven't read the hack for managing others on page 152, please do so now. You can use that slightly simpler technique for smaller projects. For larger or more complex ones, however, try this method.

HOW TO DO IT ⟩

1   Create a Memory Palace (see page 76) for the project with enough locations to fit all the steps of the project.

2   Identify the major milestones or tasks of the project, convert them to images, and connect each to a Memory Palace location.

3   Add important details for each milestone or task by using the Chain Method (see page 78) at each location. This is great for remembering names or deadlines.

4   Visualize the entire project by mentally walking the Memory Palace. "Check off" completed items by *destroying* the images. For example, I have mentally thrown paint all over

a location and its details, covered things in mud, or knocked things over so it's clear that items are no longer needed.

There is confidence in *knowing* the project. Being able to access information at any time is a huge advantage, whether you're commuting, brushing your teeth in the morning, or taking a client to lunch. Relying more and more on your memory helps in so many ways—and impresses people so much! You owe it to yourself to make the effort.

[72] Advanced: Remember Your Entire Calendar

IMAGINE HAVING YOUR entire calendar in your mind. Think of how you'd stand out from the crowd. To be able to schedule appointments, meetings, sales calls, or any other task without consulting a phone or calendar makes you look superhuman. This is a major undertaking, but with this system, it is within your ability. Many people also use the "light" version to remember their most important meetings.

THE TECHNIQUE : Person, Action, Object

To make remembering your entire calendar possible, you must have a system you know by heart. Every month has a unique, memorable image, preferably a person, and every date has an image, preferably an action or object. You imagine the month, then the date, and connect this story with the image of the activity for that time slot. It's creating a movie in your mind: This character does this action (or uses this object) in conjunction with this activity or person. In practice, it's very easy and effective—once you learn your system.

When everyone has access to our calendars on smart devices, many people question the need to make such an effort. But even if you don't rely on your memory fully, making the attempt to remember your calendar helps keep your mind sharp, makes you pay attention to your schedule, and can have a profound impact on how people perceive you.

1   Go back to the Month Memorization System hack on page 27 and do or repeat the activity. Commit what you come up with to memory.

2   Create your date system using one of the number systems described in this book. The Major System (see page 35) works best here.

3   Create your time-of-day system. I prefer Rhyme Time (see page 33). Keep in mind these number images must be different from your date images to avoid confusion. Use context to remember whether your appointment is a.m. or p.m.: If you have a meeting at "3," you will know it's 3 p.m. instead of 3 a.m.

4   Review your system several times. You should easily be able to create mental images for month, date, and time.

5   Start using your system. Create the month, date, and time images, and then connect them to an image for the event. Add details and make it exaggerated.

6   Use a backup system like a written or digital calendar. There will be times when you're sleepy, under the weather, or stressed and recall may be difficult.

7   Review your backup calendar at the beginning of every week (or day) to refresh your mental images.

8   To delete or change a scheduled event, picture yourself literally erasing the image on one date or time. You can also imagine it damaged in some way to remind yourself it is not happening the way you originally saw it, before you re-create it vividly on a different date and time. Here's an example:

> *If your original image is Santa Claus (December) hopping (9th) into your doctor's office (for your annual physical), but you reschedule it to the 8th (Santa's spare reindeer is actually an octopus holding the doctor's office building in its tentacles), change the original schedule's images to hopping*

toward the doctor's office, which has burned down.
Then be sure the new image for the 8th is extra vivid.

The more you use the system, the easier it will be to naturally remember your schedule. Eventually you'll start to be able to visualize your calendar mentally—with or without the system. In practice, I mostly use the light version of this system: I remember the current week, foregoing the month image. I turn my important events for the week into images using just date and events, as I can usually remember the times, and only focus on the upcoming week. I use the full system to remember my travel and speaking engagements for three months out.

[73] Manage Information Overload

JUST WHEN YOU think you have a handle on emails, phone calls, and deadlines, another item comes in. You can't deal with it right then, but you must remember to take care of it later. There's a memory hack for this that takes little time to set up and will quickly become second nature. Use it to make a mental note to deal with items that need to be addressed while you're busy with another task. I always recommend using your memory as your primary tool for remembering, but consider also writing notes as you develop this skill or for mission-critical items.

THE TECHNIQUE : **Your Workplace Memory Palace**

Once again, the Memory Palace (page 76) comes to the rescue. You will quickly create a Memory Palace out of your workspace with three or four obvious locations. When an item crosses your mind that you can't stop to deal with, you will convert it to an exaggerated image and connect it to one of the locations. When you have moments to pause throughout the day, you can scan your workspace Memory Palace to see what is stored in each location. The images will serve as cues to remind you what needs to be done.

HOW TO DO IT

1 Look around your work area, specifically the area in front of you to your left. Notice an obvious feature there like

something on the wall or in the corner. Note that an empty open area is not an effective location; there must be a specific item to which you can mentally attach information. Choose an item that you don't use often in your workday, so don't select your computer, monitor, or phone. That will be your primary location for your new Memory Palace.

2   Choose a second location or main item to the right of the first one. Designate that location number two. Add at least one more on the right side but still in front of you. That's location number three. Review from left to right by focusing on the item and counting them mentally: one, two, three.

3   When you're on a conference call and an email comes in that you'll need to remember to handle later, quickly convert the subject, a detail, or the sender's name into an image. Connect that image in a zany way to the first location of your Memory Palace. Quickly make the connection as bizarre as possible so it's memorable. For example, you're on a conference call and you see an email from your client named Charles. Imagine several chairs (my mental image for anyone named Charles) stacked on the plant on the edge of your desk.

4   Start the habit of glancing at all three of your locations several times a day when you have a second. Ask yourself what you see there. Take action on the items. Mentally erase them when you've completed an item. You can imagine yourself erasing them like you would a white board, or change the image to signify its completion by cutting it in half or otherwise destroying it.

This technique's power comes from purposefully drawing your attention to whatever you need to remember later so your natural memory can do its job (remember the first essential memory step: focus). Converting the information to an image and attaching it to the location in a creative way reinforces mental attention, plus provides an anchor to review if the memory doesn't pop up on its own.

[74] Win More Clients and Referrals

I WAS A top-producing real estate agent in Arizona for nearly five years and saw firsthand the importance of a good memory. Remembering well was essential to impressing people and winning referrals from satisfied clients. It's the same in any competitive business or sales environment. And let's face it—every business and sales environment is competitive.

By committing to remembering well and using the tools in this book, you too can be more confident, better serve your clients, and win more referrals.

THE TECHNIQUE ⦂ Apply the Techniques

Think of this hack as your final exam. There are many paths to being impressive in business, but memory is one of the easiest, especially with what you've already accomplished reading this book. Apply what you've learned so far to your career. Combine all the strategies and tips in this book. People will think you're superhuman.

HOW TO DO IT

1   Know the current inventory, pricing, and details. Being a walking encyclopedia of your company's products is much more impressive than saying, "I'd be happy to look that up for you!" All it takes is a daily look at inventory, improved focus, and translating numbers into memorable images. Know the details—including pricing—of your products better than anyone else. Use the memory hacks you've learned to simplify a process that others may find daunting or difficult.

2   Know names. Imagine meeting someone at a business mixer and then remembering their name when running into them a few days later at the store. Impressive! You can improve your face recognition and memory for names by reviewing the appropriate hacks in this book. The key is to make the effort. Like many things in life, the more we practice, the better we get.

3   Review to remember. My amazing real estate trainer talked about filling out tomorrow's to-do list before leaving the office at the end of the day. I suggest taking this one step further and reviewing what happens each day before you leave the office. Who did you meet? What did they look like and what were their names? Review each current prospect or client: Did you promise to do something for someone? Finally, what do you need to commit to memory about the day? Taking 5 to 10 minutes to review the day's activities tells your mind not to discard them later when you're asleep. Instead your mind will prioritize storing those details long-term.

Most businesspeople or salespeople are very similar. They have the same access to information, decent people skills, are organized, and are committed to helping people. What makes you stand out? If you improve your memory people will see you as more "with it," smarter, and better informed than everyone else. Working with you instead of your competition will be the obvious choice.

[75] Stay Sharp at Work at Any Age

IT'S NATURAL FOR our minds and bodies to change as we age. Many people find themselves slowing down mentally and physically. But we're also more experienced. We can use that experience to motivate ourselves to spend time on our physical and mental fitness to stay sharp as we get older.

The first step is to embrace the effort that it takes. When we're younger, we may be more enthusiastic because we're doing many activities for the first time. We focus better because we're both younger and more interested in new, exciting opportunities. Break what I think of as the "aging habit" and commit to a better memory at any age.

THE TECHNIQUE ⦂ Make the Effort

Let's put on our grown-up shoes and get to work. You're already strengthening your memory by reading this book. The first action step in the following section takes it to the next level, but even before that one of the best ways to stay sharp at work is to improve your physical fitness. If you're willing to take care of your body, your mind will improve as well. The benefits of cardiovascular fitness are tremendous for both the body and mind. (Always consult a physician for a plan that works best for you.) Get a plan and work it!

HOW TO DO IT >

1 Pick one section of this book and commit to learning, practicing, and using the memory hack. Master it and prove to yourself its effectiveness. Once you master it, pick another and repeat. Resist the common temptation to merely read the book and hope your mind changes by "reading osmosis." We're old enough to know that effort and practice is required for change. Benefit from that wisdom. The more effort you put into remembering, the better your mind will be. Keep in mind the adage "use it or lose it." Be willing to go through the short-term discomfort of learning a new way of using your mind in exchange for the long-term success it brings.

2 Identify why you are forgetful at work (which may be different from forgetfulness at home). Which of the three essential memory steps (FAR) do you struggle with most? 1) **F**ocus on the information, 2) **A**rrange the material in the mind, or 3) **R**etrieve it when you need it? Find the appropriate solutions in this book and use them to address the problem area.

3 Improve your mental focus. Revisit the 1-2-3 Method on page 50 and practice this method every day.

4 Don't be afraid to use notes, your smart device, or your computer as a memory aid. At the same time, stop *relying* on it. Rely on your mind and use the rest as a backup.

5 Ask yourself, "How am I going to remember that?" Taking one second to draw your attention to the situation with this question solves many absentmindedness issues.

6 Learn a foreign language in your spare time. This is a great way to keep your mind sharp, and your work life will reap the rewards of your efforts.

Mastering Memory

Many of the techniques and methods in the book seem strange the first time they are encountered. Convert information to a picture? Link it with the plant in the corner of my desk? Come on—will doing this truly improve my memory? Yes, absolutely! But you have to practice the techniques for them to work.

It's easy to read this book and think, "Well, that's pretty cool. Now I know how to remember better." It's harder—but much more effective— to put these tools into practice. Embrace the approaches even if they seem foreign. They are being used worldwide everyday by people just like you to remember better in life, school, and work.

Mastering Memory for Life

If you haven't already, pick the situation that most interests you and commit to it. Practice the technique or method for seven days. Set aside at least 10 minutes a day to improve your memory. Here are some daily and weekly activities to try.

- Memorize license plates during your commute.
- Learn the names of cashiers, servers, and anyone else you interact with regularly.
- Remember a new phone number every day.
- Review what you want to remember every time you brush your teeth.
- Every time a friend has a birthday, commit the date to memory.
- Learn something new. Pick a foreign language and learn five new words per day or expand your English vocabulary by learning one new word (and its spelling) per day.

Memory mastery comes from practice. As you develop your creativity and skill of translating difficult-to-remember material into images, your mind will change. What seemed difficult in the past will become easier, and your memory abilities will grow daily. You will feel more confident and be perceived as a memory master.

As you gain mastery, you will naturally be asked, "How do you remember so well?" You'll be ready to share your story, which I suspect is similar to mine—that you didn't have a great memory, you learned some techniques, and you improved your memory abilities.

People hunger for a better memory. You can now pay it forward by helping others. Start small by sharing the three essential memory steps (FAR). For many people, that may be enough to get them on a memory improvement path. Most of us try to multitask or don't pay enough attention when the information enters our minds and then blame forgetfulness on our "horrible memory." Encourage people to stop multitasking to help them help their minds remember better naturally.

This is especially important with our younger family members and friends. Work with them to identify which of the three steps they are having trouble with and help them fix the area of biggest concern. Play memory games with them (see page 48). Most important, lead by example. Start relying on your memory instead of your smart device. Seeing you make the effort to master your memory will inspire them to learn for themselves.

Conclusion

CONGRATULATIONS! Many people these days have resigned themselves to a poor memory, but not you. You have put in the effort, and the results are starting to show. Stay on the path and resist the temptation to revert back to any old habits (like outsourcing your memory to your smartphone or sticky notes). Your mind will stay sharp. Your memory detective will continue to reward you by "solving the case" and providing you with the memories you need when you need them!

Further Reading

Memory and Learning

The Hack-Proof Password System: Protect Yourself Online With a Memory Expert's In-Depth Guide to Remembering Passwords, by Brad Zupp

Make It Stick: The Science of Successful Learning, by Peter C. Brown, Henry L. Roediger III, and Mark A. McDaniel

Mastering the Mind

Do the Work: Overcome Resistance and Get Out of Your Own Way, by Steven Pressfield

How to Meditate: A Practical Guide to Making Friends with Your Mind, by Pema Chödrön

The Way of the SEAL: Think Like an Elite Warrior to Lead and Succeed, by Mark Divine with Allyson Edelhertz Machate

Resources for Kids

A Handful of Quiet: Happiness in Four Pebbles, by Thich Nhat Hanh

Unlock Your Amazing Memory: The Fun Guide That Shows Grades 5 to 8 How to Remember Better and Make School Easier, by Brad Zupp

Physical Fitness

Bigger Leaner Stronger: The Simple Science of Building the Ultimate Male Body, by Michael Matthews

I Love Me More Than Sugar: The Why and How of 30 Days Sugar Free, by Barry Friedman

Thinner Leaner Stronger: The Simple Science of Building the Ultimate Female Body, by Michael Matthews

Mind Maps

Mind Map Mastery: The Complete Guide to Learning and Using the Most Powerful Thinking Tool in the Universe, by Tony Buzan

Mind Mapping: Improve Memory, Concentration, Communication, Organization, Creativity, and Time Management, by Kam Knight

Creativity

A Whack on the Side of the Head: How You Can Be More Creative, by Roger von Oech

Learn Something New

Massive Open Online Courses, www.mooc.org

Khan Academy, www.khanacademy.org

Memory Presentations and Coaching

For adults: Brad Zupp, www.BradZupp.com

For students in grades 3 to 12:

Exceptional Assemblies, www.ExceptionalAssemblies.com

References

University of Waterloo. "Drawing Is Better than Writing for Memory Retention." *Waterloo News*. Accessed February 28, 2019. https: //uwaterloo.ca/news/news/drawing-better-writing-memory-retention.

Index

About the Author

BRAD ZUPP is a memory improvement expert, motivational speaker, memory coach, and author. Since 2009, he has been dedicated to testing the limits of his own memory while helping others discover the benefits that come from memory improvement. He is also a memory athlete, participating in memory competitions worldwide as his schedule allows.

Brad hasn't always had a world-class memory. When he turned 40, he noticed his daily memory abilities diminishing. Determined not to suffer a so-called "natural" memory decline as he aged, he threw himself into memory improvement and discovered that remembering better is possible.

He has been featured on *The Today Show, Fox News New York, The Dr. Steve Show*, and in *USA Today* and the *LA Times*. He is also the author of two other books about memory: *Unlock Your Amazing Memory* and *The Hack-Proof Password System*.

Brad's accomplishments include:

- Memorizing the names of 117 people in 15 minutes at a memory competition
- Setting a USA record at the World Memory Championships—two years in a row—for memorizing digits spoken at one number per second, never read or reviewed
- Memorizing 11.5 decks of shuffled playing cards perfectly in one hour at a memory competition
- Memorizing the first 10,000 digits of pi in an attempt to set the world record called "The Everest of Pi Memorization Tests"

At age 50, Brad's memory is sharper than ever. He's living proof that with a few simple techniques and a little effort we don't have to struggle to remember.

CPSIA information can be obtained
at www.ICGtesting.com
Printed in the USA
BVHW022143150519
548397BV00007B/10/P